To our wonderful Lord Jesus,
Who is more than worthy of all our love.

Printed on acid-free paper
Print book ISBN 978-1-64719-765-0
Ebook ISBN 978-1-64719-766-7

Contents

TRUTH - Part III: *Clothed Upon with Truth*

"The Lord reigns,
He is clothed with Majesty."

(Psalms 93:1)

Introduction

HAVE you ever seen the sun go down with radiant colors and felt its glory trying to say something to you? Beauty revealed in a moment's time, illuminating and transforming the ordinary. You gaze with wonder and appreciation......and then the beauty recedes.

Or perhaps it's simply hiding itself. But it leaves behind the promise of something wonderful in your heart, and somehow you feel better, even comforted for having seen it.

For it tells you something......though you're not sure what. Yet if you listen closely to your heart, you can hear it saying, *I love you, and the proof of My Love is that I'm letting you see Me.*

This is our Lord Jesus, the *King of kings and Lord of lords*, the One through Whom God the Father made the world and all that is therein (John 1:3) – *this One* has stepped out from behind the sunset and is letting us see Him.

* * *

From the beginning of Creation, the world has seen Jesus' Glory revealed through nature - through the physical things that are made (Romans 1:20).

Also, the world has seen Jesus prophesied of in the Old Testament as the Messiah - God the Father's Holy Son – and how He would come here as our Lord and Savior to save us from the spiritual authority and domination of Satan, as well as from the death-to-God effects of the Fall of Man in order to fill us with His Divine Life and thereby restore us to the Kingdom of God.

Finally, Heaven and Earth witnessed together how Jesus actually *did* arrive here, and how He paid an excruciatingly high price on a Cross to bring about so great Salvation for us.

But what do we see of Him now? We see Him revealed *in us* when we put our faith in Him as our Lord and Savior and receive His Divine Life in our soul and spirit!

And with that, now we are awaiting that Glorious Day of *"the Marriage Supper of the Lamb"* – a Divine and very *Royal* Celebration of our Oneness with Jesus through His Life dwelling within us!

But how do we live in the meantime? Is there a way we can prepare ourselves for that Heavenly Celebration? And in the process, walk in the Freedom, Power, and Victory of Jesus' Life, abiding in Him and ditching the devil, even while we're still here in this world?

Oh, yes there is, and that's what I'm going to tell you about in this book.

Cheers!

- Kathy May Hosier

"After these things, I [John] heard a great voice of a multitude in Heaven saying, 'Hallelujah....Let us be glad and rejoice, and give Honor to Him: for the Marriage of the Lamb is come, and His Wife has made Herself ready.' "

(Revelation 19:1,7)

~ 1 ~

Overture:

A Princess, a Liar, and a Royal Wedding

I'VE never forgotten the day I phoned my mother and told her how God had been speaking to me about 'Chicks for Jesus.' She was in her seventies at the time, but she laughed like a schoolgirl.

"Oh-h, what a fun name!" she said. *"I want to be a Chick for Jesus!"*

I got the same response from my eighty-six-year-old friend, Elizabeth: She laughed and said she wanted to be a Chick for Jesus too.

Their reactions are perfect examples, I think, of how girls and women everywhere responded to the chick *nom de plume* when it was first coined in the late 1950's: Young or old, it seemed they all loved it and wanted to be one.

Being a chick implied that you were feminine, cool, hip, good-looking, light-hearted, fun, desirable – you name it. If the descriptive adjective was complimentary, it was thrown into the mix with all the others.

As for me, I've always loved the idea of being a chick! In fact, I can still remember the first time I heard some girls referred to as such. I was about twelve years old, and I heard a boy at school say to his buddies, *'Hey, look at those cute chicks!'*

Quickly, I whipped my head around and saw three girls walking by in pretty dresses, giggling amongst themselves. It seemed they felt complimented to be called 'chicks.'

And I was enchanted. That innocent flirtation, so romantic and sweet, instantly captured the heart of my young imagination: A smile….the fluttering of eyelashes in the sunlight….a shy glance backward…. pink blush rising to the cheeks….everything around me all gossamer with the sound of music and the fragrance of flower petals floating in the air.

I tell you, if ever there were a little cupid of love with a red valentine and bow and arrow, he must have shot me through; because in that moment, standing there in the school corridor, suddenly I wanted to be a 'chick' more than anything in the world!

Chicks for Jesus

Honestly, though, as much as I loved the prospect of being some sort of a cool, hip chick, if you had told me back then that one day I would be a 'Chick for Jesus,' I would've felt like shooting myself in the head with a stun gun.

Because, sadly, having never been around the many smart, fun, loving, compassionate people that make up the True Body of Christ, my only Christian role models were those portrayed in movies. And they looked like mean zombies.

Those actors and actresses in all their black garb and stern, lifeless faces singing morosely about "bringing in the sheaves" really freaked me out.

On the other hand, if you had told me that:

> * I was a real princess, because I was made in the Image and Likeness of God, the King of the universe, as His very own Child

> * but the reason I didn't know it was because Satan had obscured my Royal Identity long before I was ever born

> * that just as the fairytale princesses Snow White and Sleeping Beauty had fallen into a state of sleeping death through the trickery of evil

> * so Satan had used wicked lies about God to trick Adam and Eve into bringing about the Fall of Man

* which caused them and all Mankind after them to descend into a state of spiritual death to God, and as a result, into this lower realm of life where bad things happen......

.......Honey, if you had told me all that with a straight face, I would've invited you out for coffee!

(Where I would have asked you to show me chapter and verse in the Bible to back up your claims - *as if being in a world where bad things happen isn't enough!*)

At Coffee

And let's say that at coffee you showed me those chapters and verses, and then even more, revealing that:

* just as Snow White and Sleeping Beauty's fairytale prince charmings awakened them with a kiss, and then took them off on white horses to their kingdoms to be their happy, royal brides

* so Christ Jesus - *the King of kings and Lord of lords* - came down from Heaven to make a way, through His own Life, for us to be awakened and raised from our spiritual death to God brought on by the Fall of Man

8

 * so that we could reign with Him now and forever in the Kingdom of God as His Bride; a Glorious, Divine Destiny that is ours when we receive His Life (Colossians 1:13)......

.......Beautiful friend, if you had shown me all that in the Bible, this time I would have invited you over for dinner!

Dinner

And let's say at dinner you explained that:

 * It has always been Satan's ploy to portray Christians as ignorant and mean

 * so that none of us would want anything to do with Jesus

 * and therefore would never discover our True Royal Identity, or come into God's Kingdom

 * but would instead spend eternity in a realm where the devil is dictator......

........Well, hmm.....how can I put this? Oh, I know: Do you remember that lightning-flashing ark thing in the movie *Raiders of the Lost Ark*?

Well, if you had proved to me in the Bible that all of your above bullet points are actually *true,* I would've felt like finding that ark and vanquishing the devil with it! Multiple times! Big liar.

Discovering Truth

It's been a long time since I was a young girl all turned off by those stern-looking movie actors playing the role of Christians. And yet with all my preconceived notions about Christianity, Jesus kindly and mercifully revealed Himself to me when I was only twenty-four.

Then I read the Bible for the first time, and there I learned that all of those above bullet points are in fact *true.* But I also learned that it's not my place to vanquish the devil from this world – it's the Lord's place, and one day He'll do just that!

In the meantime, my place and privilege (and everyone else's) is to *believe in* and *act on* what God says in His Word about placing our faith in Jesus as our Savior and receiving His Life to dwell within us, in our soul and spirit (which is the meaning of being "born again," as Jesus coined the phrase).

And when we *are*, then we are set free from the condemnation of sin – past, present, and future - as well as from the spiritual authority of Satan. And we can look forward to that Triumphant Day when we will join our Savior King as His 'Bride' at the Marriage Supper of the Lamb!

The Royal Wedding of the King of kings

Do you know about this Divine and very *Royal* Marriage Supper scheduled to take place in Heaven one day? Jesus described it as a Celebration of Oneness between Himself and those who have been born again with His Life!

In fact, He even shared a parable about it, saying: *"The Kingdom of Heaven is like unto a certain king who made a marriage for his son"* (Matthew 22:1-13).

In this parable, a 'certain king' invited many people to his son's wedding. Some came, some did not. But then something inappropriate and disrespectful happened: A man came to the marriage not dressed in proper wedding attire.

And when the father of the bridegroom saw this, he approached him and said, *"Friend, why have you come in not having on a wedding garment?"* And the man was speechless. Then the father ordered his servants to remove him from the wedding, *"and he was cast out into outer darkness."*

The Wedding Clothing of the Bride of Christ

In real life we've all been invited by God to be counted among the vast multitude of born again Believers who will join Jesus as His Bride at the Marriage Supper that God has arranged for His Son.

But we must be properly dressed for it. We can't show up in any ol' rag or we'll get thrown out. (Or to put it more plainly, we won't have any part with Jesus if we insist on clinging to the rags of our old fallen nature we were born into through the Fall of Man.)

So how can we be dressed for such a Divine and *very Royal* Marriage? What provision has God made for us to be clothed appropriately as: 'THE ROYAL BRIDE OF HIS MAJESTY, THE KING OF KINGS AND LORD OF LORDS'?

Ah, dear friend, the answer is beautiful: God has provided the Glorious Royal Clothing of Jesus' own Divine Life and Nature for us to be clothed with!

Jesus' Life is the *Heavenly Clothing* that God has given us to put on, that He wants us to put on, that we still have time to put on - and then *wear*, even while we are still here in this world.

Note: I use the word 'wear' there in keeping with the metaphorical language of Jesus' marriage parable. For it follows that after the guests 'put on' their wedding garments (presumably at home), they then 'wore' them to the wedding celebration.

There's the action of 'putting on' a garment, and the subsequent action of 'wearing' it.

And this is what we do after we've 'put on' the Royal Clothing of Jesus' Divine Life by being born again. We then 'wear it' by *living* in it and *walking in it* as our own, as those united in Oneness of Life with Him.

Think of it this way: When we install a new operating system on our computer, we then *use* that operating system to do our computer work, surf the internet, build a website, etc.

And that's what I'm talking about here. Figuratively speaking, Jesus' Life is the new 'Operating System' of our souls, given to us to 'live in' and 'walk in' when we are born again.

As Colossians 2:6 says: *"As you have received Christ Jesus the Lord, so walk you in Him."*

A Life from On High

And oh, what a wonderful Gift! For along with Jesus' Life being the *Divine* and *very Royal* Clothing that we are privileged to wear, it is also *Anointed Clothing,* empowering us to partake of all the Freedom, Power, Victory, and Authority of His Life within us. (First John 4:17).

Also, Jesus' Life is *Sacred Clothing,* imputing His Holiness to us as a free Gift; *Sanctified Clothing,* setting us apart for God and endowing us with His Favor and Blessings; *Invincible Clothing,* described in Ephesians 6:10-18 as.......uh oh, now I have to say it......that unfeminine 'A' word......as in the *'Ar-r-r-mor of God.'*

Oh, I know, I understand: If you're a girl - if you are of the *femme gendre'* - the 'Armor' word is hardly music to your ears. Especially since armor of any kind suggests war, and we girls are typically for love, not war.

But, actually, there's another way to look at the Armor of God. No, really, there is! In fact, in this book I'll prove it to you in a way that's sure to thrill your feminine heart, I promise.

For regardless of how we may visualize it, the Armor of God is a Biblical revelation of the Person, Nature, Character, and Attributes of *Jesus Himself* empowering us to abide in Him (John 15:4-5), bear much fruit (John 15:8), and be filled with His Might (Ephesians 6:10).

And the devil has to obey Him. Our soul's fallen life and nature are replaced by His Divine Life and Nature when we are born again. And the cloak of this world's life-sucking, Truth-twisting, God-denying system is revealed by the Light of His Life to be nothing more than what it is - the fabled emperor's non-existent clothing!

So don't let the title of this book fool you. This is not your typical chick literature. I'm not going to tell you the story of a girl who's a lot like us, and a guy who's a lot like Satan, and then give us some lame happy ending anyway.

No no, dear Sister - this is *Christian* chick lit! And our guy is *Jesus*, the King of kings and Lord of lords - handsome, strong, kind, rich, *and deeply in love with us!*

And we're going to have a happy ending in this book by seeing through the first facet of the Armor of God - *Truth* - how we can marry our Heavenly King and wear the Royal Clothing of His Life to abide in Him, ditch the devil, and be totally, Earth-shakingly, Heaven-inspiringly *gorgeous* as the Bride of Christ at the Marriage Supper of the Lamb!

~ 2 ~

A Glorious Day

"Let us be glad and rejoice, and give honor to Him,
for the Marriage of the Lamb has come,
and His Wife has made Herself ready."

(Revelation 19:7)

I LOVE how the Scriptures give us glimpses of the Celestial Joy of Heaven's Bride and Bridegroom on the Day of Their Marriage Celebration of Divine Oneness together!

For example, we read in the Psalms:

"God is gone up with a shout,
the Lord with the sound of a trumpet....
With gladness and rejoicing shall they be brought:
they shall enter the King's Palace."

(Psalm 47:5; 45:15)

And as it happened, after I met Jesus and entered into this wonderful Divine Love Story for myself, to my great joy I learned in the Bible that I had a Fabulous Future, one of reigning with Christ as part of His "Body" (that great throng of Believers who throughout the ages have been born again with His Life).

And I rejoiced that one Glorious Day, at the sound of a Trumpet, Jesus will gather us to Himself and bring us to His Joyous Marriage Supper in the Kingdom of God, where we will celebrate our Divine Oneness with Him.

Divinely Prophesied

Not everyone knows this, but the Old Testament is encrypted with beautiful prophecies of this Divine Marriage, and in the New Testament, Jesus talked about it as well.

For example, He told the people about it through the parable of that "certain king" we just looked at in the last chapter (the one who hosted a marriage for his son).

Then, after telling His disciples about the end times (which we commonly refer to as 'the last days'), He shared more about the Marriage Supper and gave yet another parable about it (known as 'the parable of the ten virgins').

Then He summed it all up, saying (and I'll conclude with the last line of His ten virgins parable):

"Immediately after the tribulation of those [last] days, the sun shall be darkened and the moon shall not give her light,

and the stars shall fall from the heavens, and the powers of the heavens shall be shaken:

And then shall appear the sign of the Son of Man [the sign of the Cross] in the heavens, and all the tribes of the earth shall mourn,

and they shall see the Son of Man [Jesus – Who is both the Son of Man and the Son of God] coming in the clouds with Power and great Glory.

And He shall send His angels with a great sound of a trumpet, and they shall gather together His Elect [those born again with His Life] from the four winds, from one end of the heavens to the other....

and they....[shall go] with Him to the Marriage, and the door shall be shut."

(Matthew 24:29-31; 25:10)

A Dream Come True

Now, I don't know about you, but when I first read about this Heavenly Marriage Supper in the Bible, immediately it became a beautiful dream in my heart that I knew was going to come true.

17

I was so filled with love for Jesus (and still am!) that it was pure happiness to imagine the joy of celebrating with all Believers our Oneness with Him on that Glorious Day!

I refer there to *"all"* Believers, because even though I'm a girl writing here to girls of all ages about being Chicks for Jesus, our Oneness with Him as His Bride is a Oneness of *soul,* not of the flesh, and therefore not of gender. For *"In Christ Jesus there is…neither male nor female, for you are all One in Him"* (Luke 20:27-36; Galatians 3:28).

In other words, the Life of Christ in the born again Believer is *Divine.* And at the Marriage Supper, after we have shed these fleshly human bodies of ours and received our Celestial Body in Heaven, we will be Divine both within *and* without!

And oh, what a time of Celebration that will be! A time when we will at last see ourselves and one another clothed with our Bridegroom King's Glory, each of us arrayed in the Majestic Splendor of the One Who gave His Life for us (John 17:22)!

A time when we will all rejoice together as Believers in Oneness with our Lord, in a Realm so High, so made of Perfect Love, it will be *Eternal Bliss* (John 17:21-23).

A time also when Heaven and Earth will behold the transcendent Glory of Heaven's Bride and Bridegroom and rejoice that Their Eternal Reign will bring Love and Joy and Peace to all! As Revelation 2:14 says:

18

"And God shall wipe away all tears from their eyes, and there shall be no more death, neither sorrow, nor crying; neither shall there be any more pain, for the former things are passed away."

Truly, as Believers, Beautiful Chicks for Jesus, we are in what has been referred to throughout the ages as 'The Greatest Love Story Ever Told,' with the most fabulous Happy-Ever-After ending imaginable!

Oh, but wait.....I haven't even told you what the name 'Chicks for Jesus' means, have I?

Well, let me get right to that! Because along with being a fun, trippy *nom de plume,* the name 'Chicks for Jesus' also has a Biblical definition, one directly from the Heart of our Heavenly Father.

And it has everything to do with Jesus as our Armor from God, as you shall see!

~ 3 ~

Chicks for Jesus

Who Are They?
And Where Do They Come From?

WHEN God first spoke the name *Chicks for Jesus* to me, I loved it and totally identified with it. By that time, I had walked with Jesus for over twenty-five years, and in my heart and mind and will, I was *for* Jesus in every way, and *against* anything that would try to pull me away from Him.

Like, anything that would compete for my affections, or purport itself to be greater than Him, or speak against Him and/or His Holy Word in any way.

So, of course, I felt honored to be thought of by God as a Chick *for* Jesus, and I wanted to be one forever!

Then, when God showed me the *Biblical* meaning of the name, I realized that, hey, I wasn't the only one that wanted me to be a Chick for Jesus!

Shortly before His Crucifixion, Jesus sat on a hilltop overlooking Jerusalem and uttered a statement so sublime, it has echoed throughout the ages with the revelation of God's Heart of Love for all of us. With tears, He said:

> *"O, Jerusalem, Jerusalem...how often would I have gathered your children, even as a hen gathers her chicks under her wings, and you would not!"*

(Matthew 23:37)

There Jesus was, the Creator of the world (John 1:3; Colossians 1:16; Revelation 10:6), speaking with the intensity of a dear mother about to die for the sake of her children!

How lovingly He compared Himself to a mother hen wanting to protect her chicks under her wings!

This reminds me of a story I once heard about a man who came upon a strange object shortly after a forest fire: Walking among the charred ruins, he saw a little mound of ashes standing bravely under a scorched tree.

Curious, he pushed the ashes gently with his foot, and lo, out came a bevy of tiny chicks, unharmed by the fire.

22

The mound of ashes was the mother hen. She had sacrificed her life, suffering the torture of fire to protect her chicks under the shelter of her wings!

Little wonder Jesus compared Himself to a mother hen just days before He suffered torture and crucifixion to save us! Not only was He going to 'become sin' on the Cross (Second Corinthians 5:21), so that He could kill it and bury it in His Grave, but at the same time He was going to take the fire of our sins' condemnation into Himself to save us from its flames (Galatians 3:13)!

Under the Shelter of His Wings

Sitting there on the hilltop that day, shedding tears over Jerusalem, ready to sacrifice His Life so that He could gather us all safely to God "as a hen gathers her chicks under her wings," Jesus was echoing Psalm 91:1- 4:

> *"He [She] that dwells in the Secret Place of the Most High shall abide under the Shadow of the Almighty.*
>
> *I will say of the Lord, He is my Refuge and Fortress, my God; in Him will I trust.*
>
> *Surely, He shall deliver you from the snare of the fowler, and from the noisome pestilence.*
>
> *He shall cover you with His Feathers, and under His Wings shall you trust, His Truth shall be your Shield and Buckler."*

23

In these verses we see our Lord God speaking to us as One with Wings, desiring to gather and protect us as His very own *Chicks* under the Shelter of His Wings!

But what is *'the Secret Place of the Most High'* referred to there in verse one? Is it a *real* place? If so, what does it have to do with Jesus? Anything at all?

Oh, it's a real place alright, and it has *everything* to do with Jesus! See if you can spot it:

He is our Refuge and Fortress (verse 2)

He shall deliver us from the snare of the fowler (verse 3)

He shall cover us with **His** Feathers and under **His** Wings shall we trust (verse 4)

Did you see it? These verses are not speaking of some building or mountaintop oasis as our Refuge, Fortress, and Deliverer – they're speaking of the Lord God Himself as being all that to us.

And this is where Jesus comes in! For *"God the Father has revealed Himself to us **in the Face of Jesus Christ**"* (Second Corinthians 4:6)!

Like Father, Like Son

Jesus is *"the Brightness of God's Glory and the Express Image of His Person....the One in Whom dwells all the Fullness of the Godhead, Bodily"* (Hebrews 1:3; Colossians 2:9).

24

And as such, God the Father has anointed Him to be *"the Mediator between God and Man"* (First Timothy 2:5; Matthew 17:5).

And this is revealed not only in the New Testament, but in the entire body of Messianic prophecy in the Old Testament as well!

Therefore, we can confidently deduce by the whole context of Scripture that *Jesus* is that *Secret Place* of the Most High referred to there in Psalm 91.

Beautiful Prophecies

But let me ask you: Why would Psalm 91 refer to Jesus in this way when He had yet to be revealed to the world, except through the many Old Testament prophecies of Him as the Messiah to come?

The answer is because the "Secret Place" referred to there is ***one of those Messianic prophecies***!

Prophetic words of knowledge from God, in their very nature, refer to that which has yet to take place, and therefore yet to be revealed to the world at large.

But now Jesus *has been* revealed to the world, and so *the Secret Place of the Most High* is no longer a secret!

And putting two and two together – combining this *Secret Place* in Psalm 91 with the *Armor of God* in Ephesians 6:10-18 - what do we see?

We see that both places represent and reveal *Jesus* as our Defense and Refuge, the One in Whom the soul of the born again Believer abides safely under the Shelter of God's Wings [metaphorically referring to God's Presence]!

And that's what I understood when God defined the name 'Chicks for Jesus' to me so long ago!

He said, *"Chicks for Jesus are those of My Daughters who abide in Christ - the Secret Place of the Most High - by wearing the Armor of God."*

~ 4 ~

The Armor of Light

"...put on the Armor of Light...
...put on the Lord Jesus Christ....
...put on the Armor of God..."

(Romans 13:12, 14; Ephesians 6:11)

I NEVER cease to be amazed at all Jesus is to us when we are born again! As the Lord and Savior of the world, He is also our *Secret Place of the Most High,* as well as our *Armor of God* – both a Refuge of Protection for us and a Dwelling Place of close proximity to the Trinity of God - God the Father, God the Son, and God the Holy Spirit.

And we are the Fabulous Bride of Christ - Beautiful Chicks for Jesus awaiting the Day of our Divine Marriage Celebration with Him!

But let me ask you: Have you ever read a love story or watched a romantic movie where there wasn't some villain trying to wreck the romance? Or at least some kind of drama threatening to destroy the love?

I hate to go all ninja on you here, but our novels and movies tend to have villains and drama because *that's the way it is on this planet!*

We're living in a fallen environment where Satan roams about trying to dominate, afflict, and destroy anyone he can, and that wicked devil has an army of evil spirits to do his bidding.

So here we are as Believers, in the midst of our time of preparation as the Bride of Christ - a time when we should be carefree and happy, singing and looking forward to our Divine Marriage Celebration with Jesus.

And what do we have in the middle of it?

Royal drama. From that un-royal, evil devil Satan and his army of evil spirits – wicked demons all of them.

As the World Turns

Not everyone knows this, but way back in Heaven, before the earth was even created, Satan (an angel at the time) became wickedly jealous of the Trinity of God and plotted to usurp Their Power and Authority and take over as ruler.

So God cast him out of Heaven, into outer darkness.

But guess what? Now Satan is feverishly working to do the same thing in this world!

Through the Fall of Man, Satan gained spiritually legal ground to influence, attack, and even dominate people whenever and wherever possible.

And he and his army of demons are still doing it (all behind the scenes of life, of course, so that people won't know it's them doing the dirty work, lest we pray to God for deliverance).

That's the bad news.

The Good News is that because Jesus is the *King of kings and Lord of lords*, He has authority over *everything,* including Satan and his demons. And when we are born again, Jesus' Life within us is *not* under Satan's authority *or* dominion.

Therefore, Satan no longer has the spiritually *legal* authority before God to influence, attack, or dominate us – because now *Jesus' Life* is dwelling in our soul!

Slings and Arrows

But Satan and his evil spirits are still a bunch of bullies - and tricksters, manipulators, control freaks, and tormentors.

And they are also liars – the Truth is not in them.

Therefore, they lie to us in every way possible, including our minds, and using every opportunity; hoping we'll believe their deceptions and thereby give them tacit (unspoken) permission to influence our thinking and behavior.

And this is why it's so important that we believe in and stand on the Word of God – which is *Truth!*

And it's also why I believe God inspired the Apostle Paul to show us Jesus' Life as '*Armor.*'

For when we are born again, the Life of Jesus *within us* is the Invincible, Divine Life that empowers us to walk in Victory over the unholy trio of *'the world, the flesh, and the devil.'*

The World, the Flesh, and the Devil

To be clear:

The *'world'* in this context is often referred to in the Bible as this fallen Man-centered, God-denying system we've set up here on Earth; also called *"this present evil age"* (Galatians 1:4; James 4:4; First John 5:19).

The *'flesh'* is a term often used in Scripture regarding the fallen nature that the human race received through the Fall of Man and its carnal effects on our minds, hearts, and desires.

And the *'devil'*.......well, we all know who he is! The devil is Satan, God's enemy, and therefore our enemy as well. Satan is the culprit who instigated the Fall of Man and thereby brought about this violent, Man-centered, God-denying, love-starved world we live in.

And the fact is, Satan and his army of fallen-angels-turned-evil-spirits are still here, feverishly hanging around in the invisible realm, exercising their spiritual power to influence, torment, lie to and manipulate people and circumstances behind the scenes of life in order to satisfy their sick lust for cruelty and dominance.

But no worries! As Chicks for Jesus destined for the Throne of God as the Bride of Christ, we're not at the mercy of the world, the flesh, *or* the devil!

Yes, this fallen world is a spiritual and carnal battlefield. But Jesus rules and reigns *over* all and *above* all!

And as born again Believers, His Life within us is our Refuge and Defense, our Power, Provision and *Victory* in every situation!

> *"Thanks be to God Who has **given us the Victory**
> through our Lord Jesus Christ."*
>
> (First Corinthians 15:54)

We have this Victory because, on the Cross, Jesus stripped Satan of his spiritually legal right over us, as Colossians 2:14-15 explains:

> *"[Jesus] blotted out the handwriting of ordinances that was against us [because of sin]...nailing it to His Cross.*
>
> *And having spoiled [evil] principalities and powers, He made a show of them openly, triumphing over them in it."*

And when we are born again, we inherit this Victory over Satan and his host of evil spirits! It's not something we must achieve for ourselves! And God confirms this in His Word, explaining that we are "complete" in Jesus:

> Jesus is *"the Head of all principalities and powers, and* ***you are complete in Him*** *"* [*by His Life within you when you are born again*].
>
> *Therefore,* ***we are more than conquerors*** *through Him that loved us [so much that He would die on the Cross to save us from the condemnation of sin and the power of Satan]."*
>
> (Colossians 2:10; Romans 8:37)

Walking in the Power of the King

Yes, it's true that Jesus said: *"In the world you shall have tribulation"* (John 16:33). But look at what He said next, in the very same sentence: *"but be of good cheer, **I** have overcome the world."*

See that? Jesus said, *"**I** have overcome the world"* [*and* the flesh, *and* the devil on our behalf]. In other words, it's the Life of *Jesus* that's the Overcoming Power within us when we are born again!

And not only was this prophesied of extensively in the Old Testament, and explained in great detail in the New Testament, but it is also spelled out for us in the seven facets of the Armor of God! And in a moment, I'll share with you how I learned that.

32

But first I have a confession to make: That is, for the first few years of my Christian life, I really didn't care for the *visual* image of myself clad in the Armor of God.

Oh, it wasn't that I didn't *love* the Biblical Truths revealed in its seven facets - actually, I did. I just didn't know them to be a revelation of *Jesus*.

Therefore, every time I thought of 'putting on' the Armor of God and 'wearing it' as a lifestyle, all I could see was me clunking around in steel all the time. Soft materials, wispy dresses, yes. Steel armor, forget it!

Besides, armor of any kind is designed for war, and I didn't want to go to war. I just wanted to bask in my love for Jesus and in His Love for me. I cherished His sweet Words in the Scriptures, and I loved thinking about Him and praying to Him.

I longed to feel His Presence each day, and to hear Him saying through His Holy Word: *"Behold, you are fair, My love; behold, you are fair; you have dove's eyes within your locks"* (Song of Solomon 4:1).

Not, "Get off your butt, soldier! Draw your sword and run to the battle!"

Love, Not War

No, I had certain aspirations for my life, and wearing steel and fighting battles wasn't among them. Forget me as superwoman or some other nifty chick with a superpower outfit; because feminine me loving masculine battle clothes just wasn't gonna' happen.

And the Lord knew that! So rather than saying, *'Away with her!'* - He helped me (as usual). And it was easy for Him!

One day, a couple of years after I met Him, He simply changed my perception of the Armor of God. He showed it to me as a wispy golden radiance surrounding me, light and airy as a feather, yet paradoxically strong and impenetrable.

Like the diaphanous rays of the sun when they encompass you: they feel lighter than air, yet they are so powerful that even pitch-black darkness cannot penetrate them or put them out.

And I was thrilled! Now my Armor was light and beautiful, and I loved it!

Little did I know that that 'wispy golden radiance' surrounding me was actually the Presence of Jesus. But I was soon to find out.

~ 5 ~

Put on the Lord Jesus Christ

*"Put on the whole Armor of God, that you may be
able to stand against the wiles of the devil."*

(Ephesians 6:11)

THE day I learned that Jesus is our Armor of God, springtime awoke
with the birds. Winter's cold bluster had passed, and delighted people
everywhere were outside basking in sunlight turned warm and golden
again.

I was outside, too, exploring the antique district of a small town
in California. Comprising several blocks of multi-storied buildings
dating back to the 1800's, the district houses a plethora of shops
brimming with memorabilia from America's nostalgic days gone by.

There were shops with antique furniture, clothes, toys, china
dishes, crystal goblets, silver cutlery, jewelry, books, tools - you name
it. If it was old Americana, one might very well find it there.

35

But I found something unexpected in one of those shops that day! As it happened, I had been browsing in and out of the various buildings when I came upon one with an extraordinary exterior.

Set back under the roof's overhang, the entire front of the one and a half story building was covered by a highly polished wood facade, expertly carved with fanciful designs and depictions of nature:

In one area, an outline of a mountain and setting sun presided over a field of giant sunflowers. In another, a jungle scene sported a giraffe here, a tiger there, and vines with swinging monkeys. A bank of trees dripped with oversized fruit alongside a river that ran through it, and abstract curlicues added a sense of whimsy to it all.

Nature abounded happily in this wood façade, captured as it were in a moment of time. Fish jumped, birds flew, a leopard sneaked, an elephant posed, all in their natural habitat of forests and jungles, rivers and streams, mountains and plains.

And as I lingered there, enjoying the fantasy and *joie de vivre* (the joy of life) portrayed in the façade's various scenes, it occurred to me that such a grand celebration of nature must surely be heralding a treasure trove of equally grand things within, so I pulled open one of the store's tall doors and stepped inside.

An Extraordinary Shop

Ah, a delicious scent of orange furniture polish immediately wafted over to greet me. I savored its sweet fragrance as I looked around, and then I stood in amazement at the sight that lay before me.

The auditorium-sized store was filled with exquisite, over-sized furniture, most pieces so large they seemed to have been built for castles! And immediately, enthusiastically, I set out to explore the aisles.

Beginning at the furthest right aisle, there I found heavy dining tables fit for a king, some long enough to seat twenty or more guests, with high-backed chairs grand enough to seat royalty.

Alongside the dining tables were massive buffets carved with images of fruit, flowers, leaves, and culinary images.

On the next few aisles, I found oversized desks, credenzas and mantles, each carved with a specific theme, such as men on horses, hunting dogs running afoot; pastoral waters with floating ducks; flowers entwined with leafy vines.

In the middle of the store stood beds with thick headboards, each carved with some kind of dreamy scene - floating angels encircled with ribbons; happy children playing in fields of flowers; a cameo of an adoring mother gazing at her baby cradled in her arms.

Accompanying the headboards were carved dressers and armoires that seemed large enough to store the clothes of the giant in *Jack and the Beanstalk.*

Slowly I browsed, imagining what it would be like to live in a castle with this amazing furniture. And when I finally reached the last aisle, I remember feeling a little nostalgic that it was all over. But then something unusual happened:

Unexpected

About halfway down the last aisle, as I was heading toward the front of the store, I happened upon a tall suit of antique armor standing in an alcove between two pillars, its body poised and ready for battle, its massive sword held high in its metal hand.

Startled, I ducked and stepped back. Dang sword, I thought it was going to come down on my head!

I'd seen suits of armor in museums before, but none were like this tall, bronzed giant! This armor was built to protect a very large man, equipped to render mortal blows with its horrid two-edged sword. And I felt small and intimidated by it.

But then I thought of the Armor of God of Ephesians 6. So, standing a comfortable distance away, I stared down the armored giant, imagining myself clad in the Armor of God, ready to go to war with this Goliath.

Bad idea! Almost immediately, thoughts of battling against such an adversary brought images of bloodshed (my own) to mind. And I knew that even if I were a huge man covered in my own armor, still I would have a hard time getting my sword past this giant's almost full-body-length shield.

Enough! I turned and headed for the exit at the front of the store. No need to wreck my happy day with thoughts of blood and swords and me lying dead on a battlefield somewhere!

But then something wonderful happened. A few steps into my escape, our Lord Jesus said in my mind:

"I AM your Shield"

And with that, I stopped and looked back at the antique armor's shield. Jesus' words were from Psalm 3:3, a verse of Scripture written into the lyrics of one of my favorite praise songs, which says: "Thou, O Lord, art a **Shield** about me. You're my Glory, You're the Lifter of my head."

'Is Jesus saying,' I wondered, *'that when we place our faith in Him as our Savior, He favors us by being a Shield about us? And is He also saying that He, Himself, **is** that facet of the Armor of God called the Shield of Faith?'*

Yes, I knew that that's *exactly* what He was saying! As Psalm 33:20 tells us: *"The Lord is our Help and our **Shield**."*

A New Revelation

As it had happened early on in my Christian life, I had memorized the seven facets of the Armor of God. But now, hearing Jesus say, *"I am your Shield"* (the fourth facet), it dawned on me that the Armor of God is a revelation of Who Jesus is within us when we are born again with His Life!

And with that, I courageously retraced my steps and stood before the antique armor to compare it to the Armor of God.

39

Starting methodically at the top, first I checked out the helmet, which covered the giant's entire head and neck area. God tells us in Ephesians 6:17 to put on the 'Helmet of Salvation.'

The Helmet of Salvation, as the Holy Spirit has since taught me, is the Mind of Christ. And by using the example of a Helmet, which covers your head, God is instructing us to *think* with the Mind of Christ when we're born again.

How do we do that? By thinking according to the Word of God! For Jesus is the *Living* Word of God (John 1:1-4, 14), and the Power of His Spirit is infused into the *written* Word of God!

And it's the Truth of the Word of God, both *Living and written,* that keeps us from being duped and dominated by the lies of the world, the flesh, and the devil!

Mighty in Battle

Next, I examined the breastplate covering the armored giant's heart and chest area, comparing it to the second facet of the Armor of God, which is the 'Breastplate of Righteousness.'

The Breastplate of Righteousness represents Jesus' Holiness given to us as a Gift by His Life within us when we are born again.

In fact, in the Old Testament, He was prophesied of as "THE LORD OUR RIGHTEOUSNESS" (Jeremiah 23:6). This I already knew, but now I wondered:

"How had I missed that the Christian's Righteousness is not only a Gift imputed to us from God when we are born again, but it's the Holy Presence of Jesus living within us when we receive His Life!?"

Moving on, next I examined the armored giant's sword. What an awesome example of that facet of the Armor of God called, *"the Sword of the Spirit, which is the Word of God"*!

On many occasions in times past, I had experienced how the laser-like Truth of the Word of God cut right through the lies of the enemy and freed my mind from deception, confusion, fear, and bad thoughts, etc.

But now I realized that I had completely missed the fact that the *Sword of the Spirit* refers not only to the **written** Word of God, but also to the **Living** Word of God – our Lord Jesus – dwelling within us when we are born again!

Something Wonderful Within

On and on I went, comparing each facet of the antique store armor to the Armor of God. And when I finally landed at the shoes, I was duly impressed!

No day loafers, these massive shoes were not only thick, but they were built up with extra metal on the top and sides, obviously to prevent the warrior's feet from being crushed under the weight of horse hooves or stabbed by an opponent's sword.

Once you can't stand on your feet, the battle is pretty much over for you. You're done. Therefore, God exhorts us to 'stand' against the enemy by having our *"feet shod with the Gospel of Peace"* (Ephesians 6:15).

The Gospel, you know, is about Jesus, "the Prince of Peace" (Isaiah 9:6), Whose Life within us gives us peace with God, instead of condemnation because of our sins.

And Ephesians 2:14 confirms this, saying of Jesus, *"He is our Peace."*

And as I stood there thinking about this, and about Jesus Himself as our Armor of God, something else wonderful happened: In my mind, the Holy Spirit said:

"Put on the Lord Jesus Christ!"

And immediately I understood what He meant: To *"put on the Armor of God"* (Ephesians 6:11) is to *"put on the Lord Jesus Christ"* (Romans 13:14) - and vice versa. The two Scripture verses mean the same thing.

And with that, I turned and left the store, practically bursting through its tall doors into the sunlight of a beautiful day. Jesus had once shown me the Armor of God as a wispy yet impenetrable golden radiance surrounding me.

But now I saw that that radiance had been *Him* all along! And I couldn't wait to get home and look up Scriptures to prove it!

~ 6 ~

Our Royal Clothing

*And Jesus said, "Search the Scriptures...
for these are they that testify of Me."*

(John 5:39)

AFTER leaving the antique store that day, I went home and began pouring over the Bible for Scriptures relating to Jesus as our Armor of God. Having read both the Old and New Testaments many times by then, I already had some verses in mind, so these I wrote down first.

Then, with the help of my Bible Concordance, I commenced my happy search for more, and eventually I found a treasure trove of Scriptures. And now I'd like to share some of them with you here.

Of course, I'd love to share them *all* with you. But for brevity's sake, let's just look at three for each facet. Three will be more than sufficient for you to see Jesus as our Armor of God, I'm sure.

Also, I want to show you something else. As I was listing Scriptures in my notebook during my happy search, I saw an image of our Divine and *very Royal* Clothing shining through it all – the Gown, the Crown, the Shoes, etc. These are all very beautiful, and so I'll show them to you under the title of each facet.

A Divine Call to Arms

To begin, the Armor of God passage opens in Ephesians 6:10-18 with a *Divine Wake-Up Call* to take our stance against Satan, not by our own ingenuity, but by the Power and Might of Jesus. As the Apostle Paul writes by revelation from God in verse 10:

> *"Finally, my brethren, be strong **in the Lord**,*
> *and in the Power of **His** Might."*

But how can we do that? How can we be "strong" in the Power and Might of Jesus? The next sentence, verse 11, tells us exactly how!

> *"Put on the whole Armor of God that you may be*
> *able to stand against the wiles of the devil."*

In other words, we're not living in the perfect world we keep hoping for, praying for 'world peace.'

We're living in a *fallen* world, which not only affects the circumstances of our lives, including our mind, body and emotions, but it's also a spiritual war zone for our souls. And this war zone is not just because of sin, but also because of Satan!

Satan and his army of evil spirits are active in the invisible realm of this world, wickedly influencing (and sometimes even dominating) people's minds to get them to act out mean or erratic behavior beyond that which they would normally act out.

And that's why when Jesus was here, He didn't always say to people He cast demons out of, *"Go and sin no more."* He understood the demonic oppression these people were suffering under.

For it's not just possessed people that are suffering under demonic oppression and influence! Evil spirits work feverishly to lie to, influence and dominate *everyone's* thinking and behavior; because evil spirits gained spiritually legal ground in the Fall of Man to do so!

Therefore, in the next verse of the Armor of God passage, the Lord tells us the hard facts of demonic activity in this world: Paul writes in verse 12:

> *"For we wrestle not against flesh and blood, but against principalities, against powers, against the rulers of the darkness of this world and spiritual wickedness in high places.*

And then God tells us what we can do about this – how we can deal victoriously with demonic oppression and influence. Paul writes in verse 13:

> *"Take unto you, therefore, the whole Armor of God that you may be able to withstand in the evil day, and having done all, to stand."*

45

Then God tells us how the Armor consists of seven facets. Listing them one by one, beginning in verse 14, Paul writes:

Stand, therefore, having your loins girt about with:

TRUTH

(Our Royal Gown)

"And the Word [of God - **JESUS**] was made flesh and dwelt among us; and we beheld His Glory, the Glory as of the Only Begotten of the Father, full of Grace and **TRUTH**" (John 1:14).

"For the Law was given by Moses, but Grace and **TRUTH** came by **JESUS CHRIST**" (John 1:17).

"And **JESUS** said, **I AM** the Way, the **TRUTH**, and the Life; no man comes unto the Father but by Me" (John 14:6).

Verse 14 continues:

And having on:

THE BREASTPLATE OF RIGHTEOUSNESS

(The Jeweled Overlay on the Bodice of our Royal Gown)

"But of Him [God the Father] are you in **CHRIST JESUS**, Who of God is made unto us Wisdom and **RIGHTEOUSNESS** and Sanctification and Redemption" (First Corinthians 1:30).

"For He [**JESUS**] Who knew no sin, became sin for us [on the Cross], that we might be made the **RIGHTEOUSNESS** of God in Him" (Second Corinthians 5:21)

"And this is His Name by which He [**JESUS**] shall be called: **THE LORD OUR RIGHTEOUSNESS**" (Jeremiah 23:6 – an O. T. prophecy of Jesus).

47

Verse 15:

And having your feet shod with

THE GOSPEL OF PEACE

(Our Golden Shoes)

"And His **[JESUS']** Name shall be called Wonderful, Counselor, the Mighty God, the Everlasting Father, the Prince of **PEACE**" (Isaiah 9:6 – an O. T. prophecy of Jesus).

"Therefore, having been justified by faith, we have **PEACE** with God through our **LORD JESUS CHRIST**" (Romans 5:1).

"In **CHRIST JESUS**, you who were afar off are now made near [to God] by the Blood of Christ. For **He** is our **PEACE** Who has...broken down the middle wall of partition between us..." (Ephesians 2:13-14).

Verse 16:

Above all, take:

THE SHIELD OF FAITH

WHICH QUENCHES ALL THE FIERY DARTS
OF THE WICKED

(Our Royal Shield)

"The **LORD** is a **SHIELD** to them that put their **FAITH** in Him" (Proverbs 30:5).

"The **LORD** is my Strength and my **SHIELD**, my heart trusted [had **FAITH**] in Him, and I am greatly helped" (Psalm 28:7).

"Hold fast the form of sound words...in **FAITH** and Love which are **in CHRIST JESUS**" (Second Timothy 1:13).

49

Verse 17:

And put on:

THE HELMET OF SALVATION

[the Mind of Christ]

(Our Royal Crown)

"But we [who are born again with Jesus' Life] have the **MIND OF CHRIST** [dwelling within us – in our soul and spirit]" (First Corinthians 2:14, 16).

"Let this **MIND** be in you which was also **in CHRIST JESUS**" (Philippians 2:5).

"For God has not given us the spirit of fear, but of power, and of love, and of a sound **MIND** [the **MIND OF CHRIST**]" (Second Timothy 1:7).

Verse 17 continues:

And take:

THE SWORD OF THE SPIRIT
WHICH IS THE WORD OF GOD

(Our Royal Scepter)

"In the beginning was the **WORD**, and the Word was with God, and the Word was God....And the Word **[JESUS]** was made flesh and dwelt among us... " (John 1:1, 14).

"The **WORD OF GOD** is quick, and powerful, and sharper than any two-edged **SWORD**...and is a discerner of the thoughts and intents of the heart" (Hebrews 4:12).

"And He **[JESUS]** was clothed with a vesture dipped in blood [His own Blood shed on the Cross], and His Name is called: **THE WORD OF GOD**." (Revelation 19:13).

Verse 18:

PRAYING ALWAYS

WITH ALL PRAYER AND SUPPLICATION

(Our Royal Access to God through Jesus)

"Who is he that condemns? It is **CHRIST** that died, yea rather, that is risen again and is at the Right Hand of God, Who also makes **INTERCESSION [prayer]** for us" (Romans 8:34).

"Likewise, the Holy Spirit [the 'Bringer' of all that **JESUS** is to us]...makes **INTERCESSION** for us" (Romans 8:26).

"Be anxious for nothing, but in everything by **PRAYER** and supplication, with thanksgiving, let your requests be made known unto God....[And] God shall supply all your need according to His Riches in Glory by **CHRIST JESUS**" (Philippians 4:6, 19).

NOTE: As the *Redeemed Daughters of the Most High,* we have been granted full access into the Presence of God, without appointment, to enjoy His Fellowship, express our heart to Him, and hear Him express His Heart to us.

This is also where we can make our requests known to God and have them answered (Matthew 21:22; Hebrews 4:14-16; Revelation 5:8).

And it's where we can speak to our King about the demons' activity in our lives, and (in the manner of Queen Esther) get them into big trouble!

> *"Therefore, in the day of my trouble, I will call upon You:*
> *for You will answer me."*

(Psalm 86:7)

* * *

And there you have it, dearly Beloved of God – three Scriptures for each of the seven facets revealing Jesus as our Armor!

And as I shared with you in Chapter 1, in this book we're going to look at the first facet - the '*Truth*' - that God has exhorted us to 'put on' and 'wear' as Royal Clothing from On High.

Later, I'll release more *Chicks for Jesus* volumes on the other six facets. And I've chosen to do it this way, because when I first began preparing the outline for this book, I fully intended to address all the seven facets in this one volume.

But soon my outline got bigger and bigger - and *bigger* - until finally I realized that if I wrote about each facet *comprehensively* in this one book, readers might run screaming from the room, and that wouldn't help anybody.

So I made the hard decision to write it all as a series, beginning with this first volume.

But no worries. Because the *Truth* that God reveals to us in the first facet is *foundational*, and therefore we must 'put it on' before we can 'wear' any of the others anyway.

Just as the fruit of a fruit tree stems from its foundation (the trunk of the tree), so the other six facets of the Armor of God stem from the *foundational Truth* of the first facet.

So it all works out for the good, as you shall see.

~ 7 ~

His Wife Has Made Herself Ready

"Blessed are they that are called to the
Marriage Supper of the Lamb."

(Revelation 19:9)

I CAN'T describe to you how comforted I felt knowing that the seven facets of the Armor of God are a guide to walking closely with Jesus.

First, because communing with Him was my heart's greatest desire.

And secondly, because I dearly wanted to 'walk the walk' and 'live the life' that He had died on the Cross to make available to me!

But there was a third reason as well. And it had to do with this one little verse toward the end of the Bible that had always given me pause for concern whenever I read it.

It's Revelation 19:7, where the curtains of Heaven are pulled back on the future for a moment, and there we see a great multitude rejoicing together, saying:

> *"Let us be glad and rejoice, and give honor to Him:*
> *for the Marriage of the Lamb has come, and*
> *His Wife has made Herself ready."*

And every time I read that, I'd be like, *'Wait...what? His Wife has **made Herself** ready? How can **I** do that? How can **I** make **myself** ready for that Glorious Day?'*

Certainly, I *wanted* to be ready when the time came for the Heavenly Voice to cry out, *"Behold, the Bridegroom has arrived, go ye out to meet Him!"* (Matthew 25:6).

As Believers and Adorers of Jesus, we all want to be ready, right?

But if we don't know what *ready* means in this context, or what it looks like in God's Eyes, how are we to know? By what standard can we determine if we're prepared to present ourselves as:

'THE ROYAL BRIDE OF HIS MAJESTY,
THE KING OF KINGS'

I mean, it's a cinch that most of us weren't raised in so much as an earthly royal family; so we haven't had the advantage of even *that* training, outward and earthly as it is.

I mean, we're not like Queen Elizabeth. She was born into the royal family of England; therefore she learned the ways of earthly royalty from childhood.

Neither are we like the late Princess Diana. As a privileged daughter of a British Earl, she grew up playing with the children of the royal family at their Windsor Castle, so at least she had the advantage of seeing the ways of earthly royalty in action before she married into the royal family.

No, we're more like Catherine (Kate) Middleton. Her parents were so-called 'commoners,' therefore she grew up learning how to be a commoner.

She lived amongst commoners, went to school with commoners, shopped with commoners, dined out with commoners. And no doubt she traveled alongside commoners when she and her family went on vacation.

And in the midst of it all, she grew up learning to think like a commoner, talk like a commoner, and act like a commoner. But when she married Prince William, she had to quit her common ways and quickly replace them with the royal family's ways, didn't she!?

And that's like us: We were born into this world with a fallen nature and have lived in that nature and learned its fallen ways since childhood.

To make matters worse, we've lived amongst the fallen and often acted out their fallen ways as well, especially those of our role models.

At least I did. I not only acted out my own fallen ways *really well,* but I often acted out those of my role models, too.

But all that changed when I put my faith in Jesus as my Savior and received His Life. I was Divinely Born into the Family of Heaven's Royalty - and wow!

The Ways of Heaven's Royalty

'Heaven's Royalty' is God the Father, God the Son, and God the Holy Spirit. And when I received Their Life, I fell *in love* with Their Ways!

For unlike the dead rules, regulations, and formalities of this fallen world's so-called 'royalty' - which for the most part have *nothing* to do with who they *really are* in their hearts and minds and character - the Ways of Heaven's Royalty stem *precisely* from Who They are!

They are *Love!* Perfect, Abundant, Immeasurable Divine *Love* to the point of Holiness (First John 4:8)! And it is the Truth graced with Their Holy *Love* that determines Their Ways - how They think and feel, receive and respond, determine and judge.

And when I began walking in Their Ways after I was born again, I experienced for myself why the Psalmist wrote:

> *"They shall sing in the Ways of the Lord,*
> *for great is the Glory of the Lord*
> *[which stems from His Love]."*

(Psalm 138:5)

The Ways of Fallen Man

On the other hand, here are a few things that God's Word says about the ways of fallen Man:

> **"All the nations walk in their own ways...."** (Acts 14:16).

> **"Destruction and misery are in their ways"** (Romans 3:16).

> **"The double-minded** [faithless] **man is unstable in all his ways"** (James 1:8).

> **"The rich man fades away in his ways"** (James 1:11).

Truly, the difference between life and death is the difference between God's Ways and the ways of fallen Man! The one makes you sing, the other eventually makes you miserable - often sooner than later.

Therefore, God exhorts us in His Word, saying: "*...turn not aside from following the Lord...for then you will go after vain things, which cannot profit nor deliver; for they are vain* [empty and worthless]*"* (First Samuel 12:20-21).

And I love how God summarizes this subject at the end of the Old Testament, in Malachi 3:13-18: There, He says that He hears those who say it's vain to serve Him, and He hears how they question the profit of keeping His Ways.

And He also hears how they call the proud *"happy,"* and say, *"They that work wickedness are set up, and they that tempt God are even delivered."*

Ah, but God hears some other people as well! The passage continues:

> *"Then they that worshipped the Lord spoke often to one another: and the Lord heard them,*
>
> *and a book of remembrance was written before Him for them that feared [worshipped] the Lord and thought upon His Name.*
>
> *And they shall be Mine, saith the Lord of Hosts, in that day when I make up My jewels,*
>
> *and I will spare them as a man spares his own son that serves him.*
>
> *Then shall you discern between the righteous and the wicked, between him that serves God and him that serves Him not."*

See that? God says He treasures us as His *"Jewels"* when we love Him and choose to walk in His Ways!

But how do we begin doing that when we've been steeped in our fallen ways since birth? Is there a Heavenly Protocol, perhaps a Divine Pattern given to us in God's Word? One by which we can *'walk in the Ways of Heaven's Royalty'* and in the process be 'ready' as the Bride of Christ for Heaven's Glorious Marriage Supper of the Lamb?

Oh yes, there is! It's the Divine Pattern of the seven facets of the Armor of God, as we've been discussing!

But learning how to 'put them on' and then 'wear' them as a lifestyle is a Divine endeavor, to be sure.

And this is where the Holy Spirit as our 'Royal Tutor' comes in....

~ 8 ~

Our Royal Tutor

And Jesus said, "When He, the Spirit of Truth, is come,
He will guide you into all Truth."

(John 16:13)

IN every earthly royal household, the children of the king are given tutors to teach them about who they are and what they have as royal heirs.

Trained experts are brought in from outside to educate them about their royal identity, their royal trust funds, their royal family's estate holdings and authority over the kingdom, as well as all aspects of royal protocol.

In *our* case, however, God has not assigned *non-royals* to teach us about our Royal Identity and all that we have in Christ! As our Heavenly Father's born again, Redeemed-by-the-Blood-of-Christ Sons and Daughters, God has appointed a *Royal* to teach us.

Who is this Royal? He is the *Holy Spirit* - the Third Person of the Trinity of God, Whom Jesus referred to as "the Spirit of Truth"!

And Jesus explained exactly *what* the Holy Spirit would be teaching us. He said:

> *"When He, the **Spirit of Truth** is come, He will guide you into all Truth...*
>
> *And He shall glorify Me, for He shall receive of **Mine** and shall **show it to you**.*
>
> *All things that the Father has are Mine. Therefore, I said that He [the Holy Spirit] shall take of Mine and shall show it unto you."*

> (John 16:13-15)

Did you catch that? Jesus said, **"He shall take of Mine and shall show it to you."**

In other words, the Holy Spirit's Divine Office as our Teacher is to lead us into all Truth by revealing to us *Who Jesus is* and *all that He has*. For Jesus is the Personal Manifestation of the God of Truth.

But the Holy Spirit doesn't then say to us, *'You can look but not partake.'* We're not like tourists who buy a ticket to, say, Queen Elizabeth's castle in England - they get to look but not touch, see but not partake, learn about what Queen Elizabeth has, not about what they have.

No, we're not looking at the things we *can't have* and *don't have* when the Holy Spirit shows us Jesus and His Kingdom. We're looking at the things we *can have* and *do have* when we're born again with His Life!

And it's the Divine Office of the Holy Spirit to teach us as Jesus' Bride how to partake of it all according to God's Word. And the 'Royal Curriculum' the Holy Spirit uses, whether we're aware of it or not, is the Divine Pattern of the seven facets of the Armor of God!

And I've not only experienced this for myself, but I've seen it in action in the lives of others. Over the years, God has given me several opportunities to become close friends with a few 'seasoned' Christians – meaning, people who had walked with Jesus for a *really long time.*

And although none of them had made the connection that the seven facets of the Armor of God reveal Jesus and how we can walk in the Power and Victory of His Life as our own, still they ended up walking in those facets beautifully!

Now, this puzzled me at first, especially since understanding that Jesus is the Armor of God had made such a difference in my own life.

But eventually I came to understand that even though these 'seasoned' Believers didn't *consciously* realize that they were walking in Jesus' Life as set forth in the Armor of God, they were doing so anyway.

Because that's what the Bible and the Holy Spirit had been teaching them to do all along!

He Shall Guide You into All Truth

If you've ever known any of these types of Christians – people who've walked with Jesus for a really long time - you may have noticed how strong their faith is (the Shield of Faith), and how consistently they think with the Mind of Christ (the Helmet of Salvation).

Also, you may have noticed how quickly they are to apply the Word of God to their situations and to rest themselves in what God says, as well as to encourage others with Bible verses (the Sword of the Spirit, which is the Word of God).

Along with all that, you may have observed how forgiven by God these 'seasoned' Christians feel, even when they fail to act out perfectly.

Why? Because they understand the high price Jesus paid on the Cross to procure their forgiveness with His own Blood (the Breastplate of Righteousness given to them as a Gift from God in response to their faith in Jesus as their Savior)!

Therefore, they don't insult the efficacy of Jesus' Holy Blood by presuming to add their 'good behavior' to it in order to earn God's forgiveness.

Finally, you may have noticed how peaceful they seem (wearing the Shoes of Peace), because they know that God will not fail to help them and deliver them, even when they may have blown it by causing their own problems.

How do they know that God will not fail to help them? They know because God says in His Word that He will!

Another reason they know is because for a long, *long* time, since the day they were born again, God has had them in Royal Training to see His Goodness to them in every situation!

This is one of the many privileges of the Bride of Christ, and God has proven His Faithfulness to His Word and to them many times over, for many years.

So even while they may not have recognized that the Armor of God is the Life of Jesus spelled out for us, and therefore they haven't practiced walking in its seven facets as such......

.......still, by the guiding and teaching of the Holy Spirit and the Word of God, they've ended up manifesting the Life of Jesus according to the Armor's seven facets anyway!

Heaven's Fast Track

So what's the advantage then of actually *knowing* what the Armor of God is? I mean, seeing that the Bible and the Holy Spirit are leading us in that direction anyway, where's the benefit?

Well, in my case, *knowing* put me on a fast track to understanding how I could walk in and enjoy all that Jesus had bestowed upon me through His Life. No longer did I have to go willy-nilly trying to use my own ingenuity to figure it out.

67

And the entire time the Holy Spirit is tutoring us through our Royal Curriculum, Jesus Himself is *with us* - walking with us, talking with us, and making the crooked places of our lives straight on this, our Royal Journey with Him through this world.

A Royal Journey?

Oh, I know it doesn't always *feel* like we're on a '*Royal Journey*.' Sometimes life in this world seems more like the back side of the desert where snakes hang out under the rocks waiting to bite, doesn't it!?

Other times it seems as if we're standing between 'the devil and the deep blue sea' - like Moses, when he led the Israelites out of Egypt, and they met up with the Red Sea before them and the Egyptian army behind them.

On other occasions, we may be so financially strapped that we feel like the Israelites in the desert, where there was no food except manna.

Still other situations can feel dry or bitter, as when the only water available to the Israelites in the desert were pools of water too bitter to drink (Exodus 15:22-25).

Even so, Jesus gives Himself to us completely as our Savior and Shepherd, Defender and Remedy in every situation - our Power, Provision, and Success......

......just as God told Moses to lift up his staff *(Jesus is our Staff of Life* - Psalm 23:4*)*, and when he did so, the Red Sea parted and the people passed through safely (Exodus 14:21)......

......and just as later, when God told Moses to make a bronze snake on a pole *(the snake represented how Jesus would become "sin" on the Cross on our behalf)*, so that when the people were doing what they oughtn't and the snakes came out and bit them, they could look at the snake on the pole and be healed (Numbers 21:8-9)......

......and just as the times when the only water available to the Israelites in the desert were those aforementioned pools of water too bitter to drink, and God showed Moses a tree and told him to cast it into the waters, and when he did so, the waters were made sweet and drinkable *(Jesus is the Tree of Life* - Genesis 2:9; Revelation 2:7)......

......and just as the Israelites continued on their journey and found no water at all, and God told Moses to strike a rock with his staff, and when he did so, fresh water gushed out in abundance *(Jesus is our Rock of Salvation, Who gave His Body to be struck and killed so that the Divine, Living Water of His Life would be poured out to us from On High (*Exodus 17:6; Psalm 94:22; 95:1; First Corinthians 10:4)......

......all these remedies given by God to Moses for the people were prophecies of Jesus, representative and symbolic of what He would *be* for us and *do* for us when we receive His Life and are learning to walk in His Power and Victory as His Bride, on this our Royal Journey with Him through this world.

~ *9* ~

Our Royal Closet

"I will greatly rejoice in the Lord,
my soul shall be joyful in my God;

for He has clothed me with the Garments of Salvation,
He has covered me with the Robe of Righteousness,

as a bridegroom decks himself with ornaments,
and as a bride adorns herself with her jewels."

(Isaiah 61:10)

AS we prepare now to open our Royal Closet, pull out the first facet of the Armor of God – *Truth* - and see how we can 'put it on' and 'wear it' to be filled with Jesus, and as His Bride walk in His Life as our own, I wonder:

Have you ever considered what our Royal Closet in Heaven will be like? The one we'll be using as the Glorious Bride of the King of kings at our Divine Marriage Celebration with Him?

71

And have you ever thought about what *His* Royal Closet will be like?

Typically, we think of closets as fairly confining spaces, don't we? And yet, as God has given me a little glimpse, our Royal Closet will not be small or confining! In fact, it won't even be like those earthly royal closets that often comprise several large rooms and an adjacent fitting room besides.

No, our Royal Closet will be in Heaven, as also will be our Divine Bridegroom's. And both will be filled with space and light transcendent in the Heavenly Realm beyond our wildest imagination.

Psalm 19:1,4-5 touches on this, saying: *"The heavens declare the Glory of God, and the firmament shows His Handiwork...in them He has set a tabernacle for the sun, which is as a **bridegroom** coming out of his chamber..."*

As the Creator of the sun, Jesus' Glory is brighter than sunlight at high noon, and His Royal Closet will encompass space and light beyond anything we've ever seen!

So what will ours be like as His Bride? Well, we can dream. But this we *can* know by the Spirit of God:

When we're in our vast, light-filled Place in Heaven, preparing to join our Bridegroom King in Holy Oneness with Him at the Divine Marriage Supper, we're going to be thrilled to finally see, in the twinkling of an eye, the full Revelation of ourselves clothed in the Glory and Majesty of our Royal Gown, our Royal Crown, our Anointed Shoes.

And we will be a Bride Most Glorious, above and beyond that of any bride the universe has ever seen.

Just as our Bridegroom Jesus is the King of kings, so will we be the Bride of brides, blest with Heaven's Beauty, Honor, and Favor above all others.

And looking into the mirror on that long-awaited Day of our Heavenly Marriage Celebration, beholding how we are clothed with the Glory of our Savior King's Life as *"His Body, the Fullness of Him Who fills all in all"* (Ephesians 1:23), each of us will finally see the Beauty of who we were created to be.

And we will be glad that we made it a point to walk closely with Jesus while we were still here on Earth. And glad for the effort we made to 'put on' and 'wear' the Royal Clothing of His Life as set forth in the Armor of God.

For even now I perceive how the Heavenly Host will be waiting with hushed tones and abated breath to see us come forth to the Marriage Supper to join our Heavenly Bridegroom. Us more beautiful than flowers, Him more radiant than the sun.

~ *10* ~

Opening our Royal Closet

*"Awake, O Zion, put on your Strength,
put on your Beautiful Garments!"*

(Isaiah 52:1)

OKAY, so let's open our Royal Closet now, pull out the first facet of the Armor of God – *Truth* - and see how we can 'put it on' and then 'wear it' as the Glorious Bride of the King of kings and Lord of lords!

And about the placement of this facet, let me ask you: Have you ever considered the significance of God telling us to gird our soul's *'loins'* about with Truth?

Why *that* area of our body? Why not some other area - like our arms or hands, for example?

Well, the answer is twofold:

First, consider how our physical *'loins'* are located in that very *personal* area of our body where babies are *conceived* and *born* into this world.

Here God is teaching us that we must be "born" of Truth in order to live and walk in Oneness of Life with Him - "born *again*," as Jesus coined the phrase, this time with His Divine Life (which includes the entire Life of the Trinity of God).

Secondly, consider how our 'loins' are connected to our legs. Here God is showing us that whatever our soul's 'life-source,' *that's* the source we're going to live in and walk in while we're in this world.

In other words, it's *personal.* The Truth that God wants us to "gird about our loins" is not impersonal, abstract, or conceptual.

It's the *Personal, Living Truth* of Jesus' Divine Life, through which we can live and walk with the Trinity of God in this world, as well as in Heaven forever.

Personal Truth

Makes me think of the movie, *You've Got Mail.* The one about a rich young businessman who opens a giant discount bookstore that quickly puts the little book shop *'around the corner'* out of business.

But he ends up with a big problem, as you know if you've seen the movie: He meets the young lady who owns the little book shop and falls in love with her.

And that's too bad for him, because she thinks he's a callous 'empty suit' and wants nothing to do with him!

So, in a lame attempt to win her over, he shows up at her door one day with a bouquet of flowers and tells her that his decision to open his store 'just around the corner' from hers was not *personal,* it was just *business.*

Well, ha, she didn't buy that at all. Practically hugging her flowers, she said, '*I'm so sick of hearing that! If something is anything, it should begin by being personal!*'

And I agree. Because people are personal, business consumers are personal, life is personal.

Even *God* is Personal! In His Word there's hardly a bit that's not presented to us on a personal level. Almost everything in the Bible is about a Personal God and a personal 'us.' (And sadly, a very personal enemy of our souls.)

Personal and Foundational

Also, we'll see that this Truth is *foundational* to the whole of our existence, and as such, it is *voluminous.* We've all seen those wedding gowns that billow out and brush against the sides of the pews as the bride floats down the aisle, right?

Well, that's like the Truth that God has revealed to us in the first facet of the Armor of God: it touches every aspect of our lives and pertains to every part of our being.

And that's what we'll see in what follows: the *very personal and foundational* Truth that God has given our souls to 'put on' and 'wear' as Royal Clothing from On High.

Therefore, we'll look at it in three parts:

OUR ROYAL IDENTITY

OUR ROYAL BRIDEGROOM

CLOTHED UPON WITH TRUTH

So let's get started......shall we!?

TRUTH

Part I

Our Royal Identity

~ *11* ~

Truth

"Thy Word is true from the beginning..."

(Psalm 119:160)

IMAGINE if some people who'd never read the Bible were searching for the Truth about their True Identity and Origin.

So they went to their local library, pulled out a Bible from the religion section, and then sat down and began reading it at the beginning - Genesis, Chapter One.

What do you think they would find?

Well, if you've read the Bible for yourself, then you and I both know that they wouldn't find a tangled mess of abstract theories and concepts on the mysteries of life all thrown together for them to decipher by their own ingenuity.

Instead, they would find the Truth *plainly* told to them in a personal, sequential, story-form way, as God spoke it to Moses; beginning with the four most important Truths God wants us to know:

1) Who He is

2) Who we are

3) The Fall of Man

4) The Salvation of Man

And if you've read Genesis for yourself, then you know that they would find that first Truth - *Who God is* - presented as a *presumptive* Truth. For the opening verse of the Bible simply says: *"In the beginning, God created the heavens and the Earth."*

There, God presents no history or scientific argument for His existence. Instead, He credits the reader's intelligence by presuming that he or she understands that there is a God and that He exists.

And this is what our Identity and Origin Seekers would see right off, in the very first verse of the Bible! There they would learn that there *is* a God, and that He created the heavens and the Earth.

Next, reading on, they would learn exactly *how* God created it all - by *speaking* it into existence: *"And God said, Let there be light, and there was light"* (verse 3).

Then they would see in verses 14 & 16 that God *spoke* the sun, moon, and stars into existence as well:

"And God said, Let there be lights in the firmament of the heaven to divide the day from the night...

And God made two great lights; the greater light [the sun] to rule the day, and the lesser light [the moon] to rule the night: and He made the stars also."

The Second Most Important Truth

The second most important Truth that God wants us to know – *'Who we are'* (our True Identity and Origin) – is revealed a few verses later, in Genesis 1:26-27:

*"And God said, Let **Us** make man in **Our** Image, and after **Our** Likeness...*

*So God created man in His own Image...**male and female** created He them."*

Right there our Identity and Origin Seekers would learn two things about God and us:

First, they would learn that God is a *Triune God* (which the Bible reveals later as God the Father, God the Son, and God the Holy Spirit).

Secondly, they would learn that we are not elements in nature's science lab, pushed around by our body's genes and subject to the survival of the fittest - as evolutionists would have us believe.

Neither are we the spawn of pond scum, or gaseous by-products of exploding stars - as Satan would have us believe.

We are the *Children of the Living God* – as *God* would have us believe!

And created in God's Image and Likeness, we have been elevated above all other earthly creatures and made dominant over them (Genesis 1:28).

The God of Truth

Ah, but not all seekers of their True Identity and Origin turn to the Bible for answers, do they? Many just send the age-old questions out into the blue - *'Who am I? Where did I come from? Why am I here?'* - and then hope for the answers to drop down.

As I did. I asked those questions, I sent them out into the blue. Perhaps you have too.

And God has answered us! *"Before they call, I will answer,"* He says in Isaiah 65:24!

And that certainly applies here; for before you and I were even born, God had already told us the Truth of our existence, beginning in the first chapter of the Bible with the revelation of *who we are* and *where we came from.*

God is *'the God of Truth'* (Deuteronomy 32:4). He *cannot* lie because He is *'Holy'* (First Samuel 6:20; Isaiah 29:19; Hebrews 6:18). Therefore, we can bank our lives on what He says, eons more than on the sun coming up tomorrow!

Mystery and Wonder

Oh, God may not tell us everything we'd like to know. Such as how a bumblebee can fly with its tiny, seemingly insufficient wings. Or how the trillions of bits of information in our cells communicate with each other to keep our bodies running as high-level, sophisticated machines.

Some details God leaves to mystery and wonder, giving place and opportunity for us to behold His Power through seemingly impossible circumstances.

Yet, just when we think God is being too mysterious, He shares some major fact with us - like in Isaiah 40:22, where He tells us that the earth is round, not flat (a fact that only in the last sixty years or so have we had the spaceships to go outside our atmosphere and see for ourselves).

But God doesn't only communicate with us through fact or mystery. As One Who describes Himself as 'Love,' sometimes He expresses Himself poetically and speaks to us through prose that stretches our imaginations and lifts our hearts to Him.

Other times in the Bible, He paints with a broad literary brush, laying out information in such a creative way that when we compare line upon line, precept upon precept, prophecy to prophecy, revelation to revelation, we see progressively deeper into the Beauty of Who He is and into the reality of His Presence in our midst.

Obviously, God is Highly Intelligent, *way beyond* genius level. In fact, He *creates* geniuses! And in His Word, His Intellect *dazzles!*

But when it comes to telling us what's *vitally important* for us to know, He tells it to us *plainly, clearly,* and *without riddle.* And this is what He's done in the very opening chapters of the Bible:

There, in the clearest, simplest language, without metaphor or innuendo, and in a way that's easy enough for a little child to understand, God tells us the first and second most important Truths He wants us to know - *Who He is,* and *Who we are!*

Next Up

Immediately following are the third and fourth most important Truths that God wants us to know:

The third is about the *Fall of Man* (Genesis 3:1-7).

And the fourth is about the *Salvation of Man*, prophesied of in Genesis 3:21, which says:

> *"Unto Adam and his wife did the Lord God*
> *make coats of skins and clothed them."*

In this tiny little verse describing great big actions, God prophesied of Jesus' Blood shed for our sins and His Life as our Royal Clothing!

We won't delve any further into these last two Truths right now; we'll just let them unfold organically as we go. The point I want to make here is that at the very beginning of the Bible, God has told us the *four most important Truths* He wants us to know:

1) *Who He is*

2) *Who we are*

3) *The Fall of Man*

4) *The Salvation of Man*

And God has revealed these right off, at the opening of the Bible, why?

Because they are Foundational to our very existence! And as such, they comprise our Royal Story.......

~ *12* ~

Our Royal Story

"When I consider Thy heavens, the work of Thy Fingers,
the moon and the stars which You have made,
what is man, that Thou art mindful of him?..."

(Psalm 8:3-4)

HAVE you heard that, collectively, we as people have a Royal Story? One that centers around those four Foundational Truths we just looked at in the opening chapters of the Bible?

Well, I don't know how much you've heard about it, but I was an adult before I knew we even *had* such a thing as a '*Royal Story.*' So you can imagine my surprise when I met Jesus at the age of twenty-four and discovered it in the Bible for myself!

And you can also imagine my surprise when I saw in those God-breathed Pages an intrinsic correlation between our Royal Story and the plotlines of *Snow White* and *Sleeping Beauty*.

You know the fairytales - royal princesses, tricked by evil into sleeping death, and then awakened to new life by the kiss of a handsome prince to become his royal bride in his kingdom and all.

Certainly, that's an overview of our own Royal Story revealed in the Bible!

You know - Royal Children of the Most High, tricked by evil Satan into the spiritual death-to-God-sleep of the Fall of Man, and then awakened to New Life by the Prince of Life - Christ Jesus our Lord - to become His Royal Bride in the Kingdom of God and all (Isaiah 9:6; Acts 3:15; Revelation 22:17).

Quite a striking similarity exists between the two scenarios, wouldn't you say? Except that ours is *real*.

Ubiquitous Effects

Yet, as clearly as the Bible reveals our Royal Story, the all-pervasive effects of the Fall of Man have obscured it in this world, as smog obscures a blue sky on a sunny day.

In fact, for the most part, it's like our Royal Story doesn't even *exist* in this world, even while we're living it out every day of our lives. Even our history books don't mention it!

As much as we need to know world history (for as they say, 'those who don't know history are doomed to repeat it'), still, our secular history books can be compared to kids recording what the other kids are doing while on a bus:

Nobody knows what the bus is, where it's going, or why they're all on it in the first place, so they record what goes on inside the bus and call it 'world history.'

But that's not our *complete* history. Our 'complete' history includes the Biblical revelation of life.

There, God not only tells us what the bus is, but why we're on it, where it's going, and what will happen to us once the bus stops and we get off.

Of this, few world historians proffer even a vague allusion. It seems the real meaning and purpose of history (God and His Presence and Purpose in our lives) has eluded them.

As it did many of the ancient Greek historians and philosophers. They viewed history as a circle, a never-ending cycle, always repeating itself yet going nowhere in particular, accomplishing no discernible purpose, and reaching no identifiable goal.

And sadly, this 'circle-to-nowhere' philosophy has trickled down to this present age and into our secular education systems.

As one professor boldly proclaimed in his inaugural speech at Cambridge: *"There is no secret and no plan in history to be discovered."*

There he was, a learned prelate, yet he had relied on this fallen world system to reveal the meaning and purpose of life to him, and he came up empty.

91

An Existential Void

Now, certainly we all could present sound reasoning for leaving a religious point of view out of our secular history books, wouldn't you agree? I mean, with so many religious views out there, which one do you choose?

Problem is, by dismissing the Biblical record of life (which tells us the *Truth* of our existence), an existential void has been established in our world history records.

And into that void, world conquerors like the Pharaohs, Alexander the Great, Caesar, Napoleon, and others like them have been portrayed as the central forces of history and the prime movers of its events, the architects of fate and designers of our destiny.

The Real Central Force and Meaning of History

On the other hand (and in stark contrast to that humanistic point of view), the Bible reveals *God* as the Central Force and Meaning of history. And the 'prime movers' under His Reign are three specific events, namely:

THE CREATION OF MAN

THE FALL OF MAN

THE SALVATION OF MAN

These three events have fundamentally shaped the thoughts and actions of all people since the beginning of life here on Earth. And in the process, these events have influenced what has gone on in this world as profoundly as tectonic plates shift deep in the earth with such force as to shape and reshape the land mass above them.

And yet they are regularly dismissed in this fallen world system!

Little wonder. Included in the Biblical record of these three events is the unfolding of our Royal Story, revealing God's Royal Identity, our Royal Identity, and sadly, the devil's evil identity - all of which Satan works feverishly behind the scenes to keep us from seeing.

But guess what? The authors of *Snow White* and *Sleeping Beauty* saw it! And they wove it into classic fairytales that have spoken to the hearts and minds of little girls for over one hundred years.

As I said to myself the first time I read God's Word from beginning to end: '*Methinks the authors of Snow White and Sleeping Beauty got their plotlines from the Bible!*'

~ 13 ~

Our Royal Identity

In spite of all the devil's lies,
I still have my Father's Eyes.

THE first correlation between the plotlines of *Snow White* and *Sleeping Beauty* and our own Royal Story is that their stories open with the revelation of their royal identity, and so does ours.

I think here of the evening I dressed up two of my granddaughters, Katie and Amanda, in fancy dresses, gloves and jewelry, and crowned each of them with a tiara.

Then I led them into our family room, sat them down in high-backed wicker chairs and served them tea and cookies while they watched a television rerun of Princess Diana's wedding to Prince Charles in England.

The girls were about seven and nine at the time, and I wish you could have seen their faces as Diana arrived at the church!

95

The gleam in their eyes and the enchanted smiles on their faces showed they were living vicariously through Diana's experience as she stepped down from her royal carriage in her buoyant white gown and floated into the great stone cathedral for her wedding.

There they were, two little girls, who just a few hours before had been running around the house laughing and playing and being silly, now were sitting upright, heads held high, expertly holding their porcelain teacups in their white-gloved hands just as daintily as any princess in a king's castle.

It seemed that royalty was in their souls' DNA. As it seems - *and is* - in all of us girls, young and old!

Of course, this is not surprising. In the very opening chapter of the Bible, we learn of our Relationship to Heaven's Royalty as those created in Their Image and Likeness as the Children of the Most High.

Which means.....*Tiaras for everyone!*

Royal Daughters of the Most High

Now, what do you think Jesus would say to all this? Would He laugh at us for thinking such high thoughts of ourselves?

No - in fact, He *confirmed* our Royal Identity and Origin when He taught us to pray, "**Our Father**, Who art in Heaven... " (Luke 11:2).

And also when He addressed men and women as "**son**" and "**daughter.**"

For example, He said to the man with palsy, "***Son***, *be of good cheer, your sins are forgiven...arise, take up your bed and go to your house*" (Matthew 9:2).

And to the woman sick with a chronic issue of blood, He kindly said, "***Daughter***, *be of good comfort, your faith [in God and in Me] has made you whole*" (Matthew 9:22).

On other occasions when He was teaching the people about the Love of God and how we should seek to love and forgive others, He said:

> "*Be ye perfect [in loving and forgiving others],*
> *even as **your Father** in Heaven is perfect....*
> *and be merciful, even as **your Heavenly Father***
> *is merciful.*"

(Matthew 5:48; Luke 6:36)

These greetings and exhortations of Jesus were not mere semantic euphemisms or metaphorical salutations. Jesus is the Creator of language, and He used it masterfully to make His various points (John 1:3).

But *not once* did He address people in a manner that would deceive them as to their relationship to God!

Jesus is the Manifestation of the God of Truth (Psalm 31:5). And as such, His greetings and exhortations taught people the Truth about their Royal Identity and Origin back then, and they still inform us today.

As God the Father said of Him on the Mount of Transfiguration: *"This is My Beloved Son...hear HIM!"* (Matthew 17:5).

Chicks Off the Royal Block

Have you heard the expression, *"Oh, he's a chip off the ol' block"* – metaphorically referring to a son who is like his father?

Well, *reverently* speaking, we girls are *Chicks off the Royal Block* (if God doesn't mind me calling Him that). And that's undoubtedly why we so often manifest the traits we've inherited from our Heavenly Father, whether we realize it or not.

And it's the same with the guys. Male and female we are all born into this world imprinted with the basic traits we've inherited from our Creator.

What *are* these 'basic traits'? Well, first and foremost, the Fundamental Nature of Heaven's Royalty is *Love*. *"God is **Love**"* (First John 4:8).

Which means that, made in God's Image and Likeness, we were made in the Image and Likeness of *Love*. And that's obviously why our lives revolve around love, whether we realize it or not.

And to me, the greatest evidence of this is that we *love* love! Why else would most of our songs be about love? *I love you, please love me too.....What the world needs now is love sweet love.....Baby, I need your lovin'.....Love makes the world go 'round.*

I daresay, if we sent all our songs out into the universe to serenade the missing aliens, those purportedly smart things would say to one another, *'Dude, those earthlings are, like, really hung up on love!'*

And they'd be right on. Unequivocally, love is a must-have in our lives.

And God knows this, because He created us this way! He created us in His Image of Love to be loved by Him above all, and then to love one another.

And whether love comes to us in the form of adoring love, or simply approval and acceptance, love is essential to our well-being.

And we *know this*, don't we!? We're *born* knowing and feeling our need for love. As babies, we all cried in our cribs until someone picked us up and hugged us!

The Innate Wisdom of Children

But there's something else we were 'born knowing.' And that is, being treated cruelly or disrespectfully is wrong and should never happen!

And we know this because our natures were designed by God to be treated with *pure love only!*

Have we fully realized this? Have we grasped the important fact that we were created to be treated with *pure love only*?!

This is how Heaven's Royalty treats One Another, and this is how They created us to be treated as well!

"How excellent is Your Lovingkindness, O God!
Therefore, the children of men put their trust
under the Shadow of Your Wings."

(Psalm 36:7)

So what happened? Why don't we always treat one another with the love and respect, kindness and manners we all crave for ourselves?

In other words, why don't we always *act* like we were made in the Image of Love? How can we be nice one day and mean the next?

Where did *that* behavior come from? How did *that* capability sneak into our natures? My gosh, sometimes we can act more like the spawn of the devil than the Children of the God of Love!

How can this be? Here we are, members of a world society that can act out good one minute and evil the next, and it's a mystery to know why.

That is, without the revelation of the Bible, it's a mystery to know why!

Therefore, to ensure that we're not among the ranks of the Biblically uninformed, let's look back to Genesis and see what God's Word has to say about *how* and *why* we got caught up in this swirl of good and evil behavior in the first place.

Oh, I know it's not always fun to 'look back' when you're in the middle of a story or a book. It's more fun to race ahead, accomplish new goals, conquer new heights.

But consider it this way: Say you were reading a novel that began with a girl stranded at sea. Immediately, you'd wonder how she got there, right?

Even when the novel went on to describe how a helicopter arrived on the scene, and the rescue guys let down a rope tied to a basket for her to get in and get pulled up into the helicopter, chances are you'd still wonder:

'How did she get stranded at sea in the first place? Was she swimming and got swept away in an undercurrent? Was she fishing and her boat capsized? Did she parachute out of an airplane and miss her landing spot?'

Until you knew the answer, you might find it hard to settle down and enjoy the rest of her story, right? In fact, you might even find the novel frustrating until you learned the answer.

So I've been talking about how we were made in the Image of Love. But that begs the question *Why? Why* are we all capable of acting out in ways *not* based on love?

Oh, you probably know the answer to that already. I believe you're smart and lovely, and probably very Biblically educated.

But do you remember how God told Moses not to lead the Israelites out of Egypt any faster than the young and aged could travel? Not running over them and leaving them in the dust?

Well, that's the pace God has put on my heart to keep in this book. He doesn't want any Biblical information to run over the heads of those who may not yet know His Word very well (or at all).

So, for their sake, let's slow our roll and take a moment to look at a short synopsis of our Royal History and see what God's Word has to say about why we can act out good one minute and bad the next. Then we'll all know.

~ 14 ~

A Short Synopsis of Our Royal History

IN THE BEGINNING, after creating the heavens and the Earth, our Royal Triune God - God the Father, God the Son, and God the Holy Spirit - said: *"Let Us create man in Our Image, according to Our Likeness..."* (Genesis 1:26).

"So God created man in His own Image, in the Image of God created He him; male and female created He them" (Genesis 1:27).

Thus, Adam and Eve, the first of Mankind, became the Royal Children of the Most High.

But something terrible happened in the Garden where they were created: Satan tricked them into dying to God. And he used one of their greatest gifts from God to do it - their free will.

The Freedom to Choose

Yes, God gave Adam and Eve a free will with which to make their own choices, moral and otherwise. He didn't want little Pinocchios - even Japetto wasn't satisfied with a wooden robot for a child. And just like Japetto, God wanted His Children to be real in every way as well.

Therefore, He not only made them in His Image and Likeness, but since He has a free Will, He gave them a free will as well, without which they would simply be robots.

And their free will came with no strings attached, right down to having the freedom to choose to love God and believe His Word, or not.

But their free will also came with grave danger! For to be truly free they had to be exposed to everything, including the existence of evil.

They had to, otherwise they wouldn't really be free to make their own choices about real life in a real universe, as God is.

And it was on this very point that Satan *tricked* them. And he did it by leading them to a point where they had to make a choice between believing what he said, or what God said.

And Satan used *"The Tree of the Knowledge of Good and Evil"* that was in the Garden to do it!

A Moral Dilemma

From the beginning, God told Adam and Eve the Truth about that tree, warning them not to eat the fruit of it – *"For in the day you eat of it, you shall die,"* He told them (Genesis 2:17).

But then along comes Satan, saying to Eve, "You shall not die, for God knows that in the day you eat thereof, you shall be **as God**, knowing good and evil" (Genesis 3:4).

Right there, Satan basically calls God a liar! (As Satan and his demons are still doing today in the minds of people the world over!)

But God is *"the God of Truth"* (Isaiah 65:16), Who cannot lie. And God is also *"Love"* (First John 4:8), and He loved Adam and Eve beyond imagination.

So, *of course,* He told them the Truth as to what would happen to them if they ate the fruit of that good and evil tree!

In fact, He even *commanded* them not to eat it! All loving parents teach their children about danger. *'Don't run into the street - you'll get hit by a car!'*

And God is the best Parent in the universe! Therefore, He said to them, *"Of every tree of the Garden you may eat freely; but of the Tree of the Knowledge of Good and Evil, you shall not eat of it: for in the day that you eat thereof, you shall surely die"* (Genesis 16-17).

But God was not talking about them dying *physically* - at least not immediately. He was talking about them dying to *Him* - to eternal life with *Him* - for *He is* Eternal Life!

An Existential Reality

But that begs the question: 'What was so bad about that forbidden fruit in the first place?'

The answer in its simplest form is this: To *eat it* was to *become it.* To eat the good and evil fruit was to *become* good and evil.

Just as the Tree of Life in the Garden (of which God encouraged them to eat) had the power to procreate eternal life in the soul of the one who ate of it (Genesis 3:22-24)......

.......so the forbidden tree had the power to procreate its good and evil nature in the soul of the one who ate of it as well!

And that's the tragedy of the Fall of Man: Since God's Nature is LOVE, and the nature of evil is HATE - the extreme opposite of God's Nature - Adam and Eve could not have God's Spirit living in their spirit if evil became part of their soul.

And *that's why* God commanded them not to eat the good and evil fruit!

But Eve ate it anyway. And she gave some to her husband, and he ate.

When the temptation for self-elevation came, they chose to believe the devil's word over God's Word. And so they ate......and died to God.

Falling

Oh, the horror they must have felt when their innocence died, when their minds were infiltrated with good and evil thoughts, and they were now capable of good and evil acts toward God and one another.

They had expected to rise, but instead they fell......down, down, down, into a lower nature. As in a bad dream, where one is falling into an abyss, they fell into a nature capable of doing not only good things but *bad* things - evil things, mean things.

Things that are the opposite of love - like lying, cheating, stealing, backbiting, all forms of abuse, including hate and murder.

And, oh, who knows what grief they experienced when the Glory of God that had surrounded them as clothing was now gone, and they found themselves naked.

Who knows how ashamed, vulnerable, and exposed they felt as they hid from God and tried to make clothes of leaves to cover themselves (Genesis 3:7-8).

For not only was their likeness to God now marred and their High State of Existence now lost, but due to the evil capabilities now residing in their fallen nature, they were experiencing the reality that they were now separated from a Life-Union with God.

And no doubt now, *finally,* they understood *why* God had told them not to eat the forbidden fruit.

But it was too late. They had eaten it anyway. Satan had instigated within them a desire for self-exaltation, and so they ate, unaware that while they chewed and swallowed....and died to God....the devil was already planning his victory celebration.

~ 15 ~

Liar, Liar, Pants on Fire

*"And the serpent said to the woman,
'You shall not surely die.'"*

(Genesis 3:4)

AND there we have it – there is the second correlation between our Royal Story and the fairytales *Snow White* and *Sleeping Beauty*.

The first, you'll recall, is that their princess stories open with the revelation of their royal identity, and so does ours.

The Bible reveals in its opening chapter that we were made in the Image and Likeness of Heaven's Royalty!

The second correlation, which we just saw, is where they were tricked by evil into sleeping death, and so were we! Tricked by evil Satan into the spiritual death-to-God sleep of the Fall of Man. As Romans 5:12 tells us:

*"Wherefore, as by one man [Adam], sin entered the world, and death by sin, **so death passed upon all men**, for all have sinned."*

The difference, however, is that Snow White and Sleeping Beauty got to be unconscious during their death-sleep, whereas we are awake during ours.

And being awake, Adam and Eve must have known immediately that Satan had lied to them!

Certainly, it couldn't have been too long before they realized that the forbidden tree was not designed to elevate but to *procreate* its good and evil nature in those who ate its fruit.

Because immediately they ate of it, the nature of their soul (their 'Me, Myself and I' living inside their bodies) became exactly that - good *and* evil.

Fruit of its Own Kind

Now, some people might think: 'So what? So they ate from the Tree of the **Knowledge** of Good and Evil - big deal! What's so wrong with **knowing** about evil? Didn't that forbidden tree simply produce the *intellectual* knowledge of evil?'

Nope. The root of that Hebrew word 'knowledge,' as it is used there in Genesis 2:17 to describe that forbidden tree, was not derived from the *intellectual* form only, as in a mental comprehension of something.

Rather, it was derived from a two-pronged form - one denoting the *intellect,* and the other referring to the *procreative* (as when a man 'knows' his wife in the marriage bed and a child is procreated of their union).

And that's a completely different way than God knows about evil!

The Knowledge of the Holy

Yes, God *intellectually* knows about evil. No doubt His Omniscient (all-knowing) Mind comprehends evil to its furthest degree. But still, He remains Holy!

Why? Because His knowledge of evil is not *intimate.* God has never taken evil *into* Himself and become *one* with it.

And conversely, evil has never procreated itself in Him.

But it did in Adam and Eve! They took the 'good and evil' fruit *into* themselves, and their souls became exactly that - good *and* evil.

As a result, now they would think not only *good* thoughts and demonstrate *good* behavior, but they would think *bad* thoughts and demonstrate *bad* behavior as well.

In other words, now they were capable of acting out *both ways,* as all people would be after them.

But God doesn't act out both ways! God is Perfect Love and Goodness to the point of Holiness ("devoid of evil," as the dictionary defines 'holiness').

Evil, on the other hand, is mean, hateful, cruel, unforgiving, and merciless – the very *opposite* of God's Holy Nature of Love.

And *that's why* the nature of evil can have no Oneness with God, no Life-Connection to Him.

And Satan knew this all too well when he lied to Eve.

~ 16 ~

Me, Myself, and I

She stood in the Palace of Wurtzung,
in the Hall of a Thousand Mirrors.
A thousand hands stretched out to meet her,
a thousand smiles greeted hers.
A thousand eyes would weep if she wept.
But they were all her hands, her smiles, her tears.
She knew not that she was lost in the solitude of Self,
neither did she care.

ONE of the characteristics of evil is that it's totally *Self*-centered - narcissistic to the max. And I'm sure that when Adam and Eve ate the good and evil fruit, they had no idea that they were turning the needle of their soul's compass from God to 'Self' in the process.

But that's what they did! In their tragic effort to ascend and be 'as God' (as the devil said they would), the opposite happened:

Instead of ascending to God's Nature, which is 'altero-centric' (*others*-centered), they *descended* into a nature that is 'centripetal' (*self*-centered).

And to use geomagnetism as an illustration, 'Self' turns automatically inward to its own magnetic plane; to the magnetic meridian of seeking its own interests, often above all else.

Even when Self reaches out to love and give to others, if there's not a little love, or at least some respect or consideration coming back in return, Self easily grows cold - and sometimes even stops loving altogether. Self can even get mean when neglected.

But God doesn't get mean, even when He's neglected or rejected (as Jesus demonstrated all the way to the Cross). Being Perfect Love, God's Nature goes *outward,* freely loving and seeking the good of His Creation without turning inward or becoming cold and mean when He's not loved and appreciated in return.

Oh, I'm not saying that God doesn't *hate* evil, or that because He is Love, He can be manipulated and/or treated disrespectfully (except when it's part of His own Purpose and Plan - like, for example, the Cross of Christ).

Outside of that, however, God dwells in Light *unapproachable* by disrespect, baseness, and wickedness.

Yes, He deals with evil (usually by delivering us from it, often waiting until we're *ready* for Him to deliver us!). Yet, because He loves us, He is kind and tender, and greatly rejoices when we love Him in return.

God's Others-Centered Nature is Love

God is continually working to bring good into our lives, even to the point of hurt to Himself (dramatically demonstrated by Jesus on the Cross).

But whether we love Him in return or not, His 'Others-Centered' Nature never changes; never turns inward to be dominated by selfish interests, never gets mean.

God is the Source and Fountainhead of all Love, and He says, *"I am the Lord, I change not; therefore...you are not consumed"* (Malachi 3:6).

And that's the irony of the Fall of Man: In seeking to become like God, Adam and Eve did something illogical: They did the *opposite* of what God had told them to do - they ate from the forbidden tree rather than from the Tree of Life.

And, honey, that's not even rational! I mean, one can't expect to be *like* God if one does the *opposite* of what He says to do! Mere common sense tells us that, right?

Sane logic tells us that if we want to be 'like' someone - say, our sister, for example - then we say what she says, do what she does, go where she goes.

We don't do the *opposite* and then expect to be 'like' her.

But that's what Adam and Eve did! They did the *opposite* of what God said to do, and then expected to be like Him – 'as God.'

115

So were Adam and Eve irrational people? Were their natures intrinsically warped so as to produce illogical thinking and actions?

No, not at all, because before they ate the good and evil fruit, they still possessed the High Estate into which they were created. Which means that they were far greater, smarter, and *saner* than they were after the Fall, of that we can be sure.

It's just that they were dumb as rocks about evil! Before Satan came along, they didn't even know what a lie *was*, because up to that point they'd heard only Truth, as God speaks only Truth. Therefore, the possibility of a lie wasn't even in the data banks of their minds.

Blindsided

So when Satan approached Eve in the Garden and told her that she would not die if she ate the good and evil fruit (as *God* said she would), she was faced with her first lie. *And* with making her first moral choice:

Whom would she choose to believe? God? Or Satan, who was promising her something that seemed ultimately beneficial to *her*? Something that promised to elevate *her*?

Well, we all know what she did. She chose to believe Satan over God. And so did Adam. Thinking to elevate themselves, they ate the forbidden fruit.

With great expectations they swallowed it, little knowing that instead of rising to the status of their Others-centered God, their souls would tragically descend into a Self-centered, Self-revolving meridian of '*Me, Myself, and I*' - a slippery slope leading to narcissism rather than to God. Which is precisely what is meant by the term 'The *Fall of Man.*'

Once Adam and Eve chose to disobey God (in an effort to be the god of their own Identity), their descent into Self was complete: their spirits were empty, the lights were out.

The Meaning of Life

They say that the most common questions people ask are those age-old ones – "*Who am I? Where did I come from? Why am I here on this planet?*"

Before we are born again with the Life of Jesus, our spirit's emptiness of the Presence of God is felt by each of us on such an innate level that we often describe it as 'that empty hole inside.'

I felt that empty hole, even as a child. Eventually, as a young woman, I would look into the night sky, gaze at the stars under the light of a propitious moon and send those same age-old questions out into the universe: "*Who am I? Where did I come from? Why am I here on this planet?*"

I asked those questions, not out of curiosity, but because I felt the disturbing reality of being disconnected from that 'Something Greater' that I sensed in the universe, a 'Something Wonderful' to which I instinctively knew I should be connected.

Also, I asked those questions because I knew there was more to me than what appeared on the surface. I could feel a Greater Identity deep within the recesses of my being, yet I could not express it or put my finger on exactly what it was.

~ 17 ~

Then I Hear My Name

When the stars come out at night,
when the sun sends forth its light,
then You call my name.

(Adapted from 'Under the Rain' by Stoker)

BEFORE I met Jesus, I had no idea why my great desire to be loved took precedence over all my other desires, or why it was such a motivating factor in my relationships with people.

I know now, of course, that it was evidence I was created in the Image of Love, to be in a Living Relationship with our God of *Love*.

A second evidence that we were created in God's Image is that He is *"the God of all Comfort"* (Second Corinthians 1:3), and we need comfort, sometimes desperately. We were *born* needing comfort. As babies we all cried in our cribs until someone picked us up and hugged us and comforted us, right?

The third evidence that we were created in God's Image is that He is the Creator of all Beauty (Genesis 1:1; John 1:3), and we love beauty. Real beauty can move us to tears and inspire our souls to embrace it. Like how I feel every time I visit Big Sur......

Where Beauty and Power Play Together

As you may know, Big Sur is a forty-mile or so mountain range in Northern California that stands majestically alongside the beauty of the sea.

The south end is replete with lovely forests and open hillsides of flora, and here weary travelers rest at Big Sur Lodge, and happy campers pitch their tents beside the wide river that runs through it.

Nature-lovers hike the trails, and the adventurous visit the local stable and go horseback riding along the bluffs. Nearby, on Andrew Beach, artists paint at their easels and delighted children play at the water's edge.

Truly, Big Sur south is a delight to all who visit it, and I love every minute I am there. But my heart *longs* for Big Sur north......

Majestic

Ah, Big Sur north, where the mountain range often drops off abruptly above the water, revealing rugged walls of rock and compressed dirt that stand like impenetrable fortresses between land and sea.

Sometimes, though, the land slopes down less formidably. But whether steep or sloping gently, the mountain range always weaves in and out of the water like lace on the edge of a skirt, in the process forming little beaches for sunbathers and rock castles strewn out to sea for the birds and mammals to congregate.

Highway One runs along the precipice of it all, flanked on one side by the mountain range, and on the other by the vast expanse of ocean.

God says, *"Heaven is My Throne, and Earth is My Footstool"* (Isaiah 66:1). And traveling along Highway One, the view offers a sense of the magnitude of God:

It is *majestic*, and it is *big* - like God. BIG sky, BIG mountain range, BIG ocean. And I always feel I'm getting a little glimpse of Heaven's Royalty expressed in nature whenever I am there.

A Glimpse of the Glory of God

The Old Testament records how certain people had the privilege of glimpsing the Glory of God in nature.

Like the prophet Ezekiel, for example. He wrote: *"His Voice was like a noise of many waters, and the Earth shines with His Glory"* (Ezekiel 43:2).

Other Old Testament prophets had visions of God sitting on His Throne, high above the Earth, His Glory shining down on it. Such as King David, who wrote:

"The Voice of the Lord is upon the waters: the God of Glory thunders [and what creature under the sun is not subdued by a good thunderstorm!?]*....the Voice of the Lord is powerful...and full of Majesty....The Lord sits upon the flood; yea, the Lord sits King forever"* (Psalm 29:3,4,10).

Such visions of God's Glory are ever imaginable to me in Big Sur north, where land and sea embrace to give us a tiny glimpse of the Beauty and Power of our Creator.

Traveling along Highway One, high above the ocean, the alchemy of breathtaking perspectives washes over my being and lifts my consciousness. I love every fresh view around every bend in the road. And by the time I arrive at my favorite turn out and get out of the car, I am overcome with a sense of the *vastness* of God.

So I sit on the edge of the cliffs and watch the ocean move with the tides and sparkle with the sunlight dancing over its surface. Sailboats bob on the horizon like children's toys, and seagulls call out as they ride the winds.

I close my eyes and lift my face to the sun......the breeze touches my hair. Below me, spent waves whish among the rocks awhile before returning from whence they came......and time is no more. I am in Elizabeth Browning's poem:

"The little cares that fretted me, I lost them yesterday,
among the fields above the sea, among the winds at play."

(Out in the Fields with God)

I breathe deep, trying to take it all into myself. I am drawn to it, as if it is calling my name, saying, *"You were meant for all this. God created you to be filled with Himself - His Life, His Beauty, His Power."*

So I breathe deeper. My body relaxes; my soul expands with the oxygen of inspiration; my spirit.......uh, my spirit.......well, hmm, what's up with that?

~18 ~

The Spirit of Man

"The Lord will perfect that which has to do with me:
Your Mercy, O Lord, endures forever:
forsake not the work of Your own Hands."

(Psalm 138:8)

I DON'T know how much you've heard about the spirit of Man, but I grew up occasionally hearing my mother and her sisters talk about 'spirituality,' and about how 'spiritual' this person or that person was becoming.

And while I always listened to them respectfully, my secret opinion was that such discussion about our spirit was nothing more than conjecture about the unknown.

I believed it impossible for us to know anything substantive about something so elusive as our spirit – because my experience was that of a two-part being: I had a body, and I had a soul. Nobody had to educate me about that. I was highly aware of my body and intimately acquainted with my soul (that Me, Myself, and I living inside my body).

These two parts practically screamed at me for attention every day. And still do! My body says, *'Feed me, wash me, I'm cold, I'm hot, I'm sleepy, I have a headache, oh, now it's gone, I feel good.'* I have only to stub my toe to elicit intense fellowship with my body.

As for my soul.....well, except when I'm sleeping, I let myself know exactly how I feel and what I want every minute of every day. And if I'm not making myself happy, I let myself know all about it!

I'm sure you can relate. Undeniably, there's a living, breathing soul within all of us. Of this we can be sure because it's......well, it's *you* and it's *me*......living inside our body.

Our Spirit

But our spirit? What's up with *that*? Can we say that we know our own spirit in even a miniscule way compared to what we know of our body and soul?

I mean, if we really *were* created with a spirit (which we *were*, because God said so), why then don't we *experience* it in somewhat the same volume as our *very outspoken* body and soul?

Only in the Bible can we find the real answer. There, God reveals through the whole context of Scripture that our spirit is the place where we were meant to be connected in Oneness to Him - by His

Spirit living in our spirit. But the Fall of Man broke that connection, as we've seen.

Of course, some people might think, '*So what if I wasn't born with God in my spirit? Big deal, how can that possibly affect my life in the here and now?*'

Natural questions, those. Our spirit - that seemingly silent and elusive part of our being - is like *so not there* to our senses, it's easy to think that it's separate and distinct from our experiences in this world.

Or that, at the very most, our spirit's effect on our lives in the 'here and now' is little more than negligible.

But to use an oxymoron, that's neither Biblical nor true. Our lives are greatly influenced and held in the balance by what goes on with us spiritually, whether it's the beautiful influence of God on our spirit, or the negative influence of the devil.

And how we respond to either greatly determines how we roll, now and forever.

Precious to God

But one of the many wonderful things about our Heavenly Father is that even though we lost our spiritual connection to Him in the Fall, that doesn't mean He ditched us. We are still His precious Children.

And we saw this earlier through Jesus teaching us to pray, *"Our Father, Who art in Heaven."*

127

And to make sure we didn't miss it, He repeated it again at His Ascension, saying, *"I ascend unto My Father and your Father, to My God and your God."*

Clearly, Jesus wanted us to understand that we are still God's precious Children, imprinted with His own Image and Likeness.

And if you were anything like me as a child, you felt that Imprint and you knew that *'who you are'* on the inside is greater than what appears of you on the surface.

Regardless of your circumstances or how you may have been treated, you felt significant, even valuable, and you hated it when someone treated you less than that.

A Feeling of Significance

In spite of what happened to us in the Fall, there remains within each of us a latent memory of the Glory and Dignity for which we were created; a strong witness that we are greater and more important in the grand scheme of life than what appears of us now.

And the Bible confirms that witness! Regardless of how it has been put down, scoffed at, and outlawed over the centuries, the Bible offers the only true explanation of our feelings of value and significance (and sometimes even of grandeur).

In those Holy Spirit-breathed pages, we learn that we are not swamp spores evolved into the highly intelligent, amazing beings we are now. We were complete and perfect and amazing to begin with!

Right off, God created us as His very own Children, in His very own Image and Likeness, with a Divine and very *Royal* Lineage that can be traced directly back to Him (Genesis 1:26-27)!

The reason it just seems so fantastic that we really-truly-could-be-the-actual-bona-fide-honest-to-God-real 'Children of the Highest' is that God is Divine, and we're not.

Dust and Deity

But what we see of ourselves now, after the Fall, is not the fullness of what we were created to be! We were created to contain *God*. To be filled with the Divine Presence of the Trinity of *God* in our spirit.

And instead of having a good and evil nature in our soul, we were created to have *God's* Nature in our soul - God and us expressed through our physical being in this world, a uniting of dust and Deity.

If only we knew from whence we came......

To use a metaphor of the sea, God is the Ocean, and we are the Droplets of it. And though we were cast upon the shore and absorbed by the sand into a darker, drier, *harder* existence than that for which we were created, that doesn't change who we are. We belong to the Sea. We belong to God.

And so we ask the same age-old questions: *'Who am I? Where did I come from? Why am I here on this planet?'* God has stamped His Image onto our souls and given us a spirit - a place where He could live within us, and where we could be united in Oneness with Him.

And though we lost that capacity in the Fall, still He is our Ocean, the Meaning of our lives. And we, the Droplets, will never be complete until we are restored to Him.

Never mind what Satan (*"the father of lies"* - John 8:44) wants us to believe about ourselves. We, the Beloved Children of God, really do have a Glorious Identity, latent as it is within us.

We may not know how exalted our existence was meant to be - before the Fall. Or how High and Glorious we might have been without that tragic event.

Nevertheless, our souls have been imprinted with the Image of *God*. And try as the devil has, that wicked instigator of the Fall of Man has not been able to obliterate it.

~ 19 ~

While You Were Sleeping

"O bless our God,
Who holds our soul in life."

(Psalm 66:9)

DID you ever wonder what was going on with Snow White and Sleeping Beauty while they were sleeping? Were they dreaming? Did they have any subconscious thoughts at all? Or were they just dead, with no mental or soul activity whatsoever?

Well, whatever was going on with them, 'We the People' are still conscious and experiencing active lives during our state of sleeping death to God.

Because of His great Love for us, God has breathed enough life into our bodies and souls to give us time to seek Him and be reunited with Him before we physically die.

131

Now, only *God* can perform a miracle like that! Only *God* can do the impossible, like letting us have a conscious life, even while we are dead to Him, the Source of all life.

And I think it was the sweetest Love of God for Adam and Eve that kept Him from taking them out after the Fall and making a new couple that would honor Him by believing His Word over Satan's.

As the saying goes, *'Don't give me that look, boy! I brought you into this world, and I can take you out and make another that looks just like you!*

God could have done that to Adam and Eve. But He didn't. He loved them too much. And the fact that He doesn't do that to all of us today is because He also loves *us* too much. He wants to *save* us, not replace us. We are each exceedingly precious to Him.

Of Immeasurable Worth

I think here of a story I once heard about a devout pastor who used an unusual method when trying to explain to a group of people their value to God:

He took a twenty-dollar bill out of his wallet, crumpled it up, threw it on the ground, and then stomped it into the dirt. Then he picked it up, brushed off the dirt, and held it up to the people.

'How much is this bill worth?' he asked them.

'Twenty dollars,' they answered.

'Right,' he said. *'And just as this badly treated twenty-dollar bill is still worth its original value - twenty-dollars - so, regardless of what has happened to you and what you've been through, you are worth every bit as much to the Heart of God as the day He created you.'*

And amen to that! Because that's what God tells us in His Word! In every way possible, He communicates to us that regardless of the Fall and what has happened to us in life, or what we've done, we are still precious to Him.

And He doesn't want to replace us, He wants to save us. He doesn't want to throw us away, He wants to keep us. We are still His own Children, and He loves us beyond what we can imagine.

Environment

To me, the fact that that pastor would have to mess up a twenty-dollar bill to demonstrate his point about how much God loves us is very telling. For one thing, it reveals that we were *not built* for this fallen world, where God seems so far away, and where we hurt one another with the evil part of our fallen natures.

And for another, it reveals that we were made for *love only,* created to be loved by our God of Love, and to love Him in return, and then to love one another with His Love.

And built this way - for love only - we were not equipped to live in this fallen environment, where not only goodness but badness, shame, mocking, and insults are served up as 'normal.'

Neither were we built for an environment where deceit, misunderstandings, and lack of love often afflict our relationships and circumstances; and where Satan and his demons stalk around in the unseen realm, insulting us in our own minds and looking for ways to attack us and hide our True Identity from us.

The environment we *were* built to live in was a gloriously happy one, described in Genesis 2:8 as a *"Garden"* - a paradise of Love and Peace and Joy, with the Lord of Love walking among us under an open Heaven (Genesis 3:8).

And that's why, to me, we're never totally comfortable in this fallen world, like the fabled princess in '*The Princess and the Pea.*'

The Princess and the Pea

If you've read this fable, you know that one day while the princess was outside, exploring the fields and forests, she ended up getting lost in a neighboring province.

Well, lucky for her, after wandering around awhile, she met up with a handsome young prince on horseback.

He was the prince of the province she'd wandered into; and as they talked and laughed and became acquainted, he fell in love with her and wanted to marry her.

So he invited her home to meet his parents, the king and queen, and to stay with them in their castle while he searched for her parents.

A Royal Test

Now, the queen liked the girl alright, seeing that she was well-mannered and had that certain *'je ne sais quoi'* of a well-bred princess. But learning that her son wanted to marry her, the queen had to make sure she was really a princess.

So she ordered the servants to place a dried pea at the bottom of the guest bed and then stack it high with many feather mattresses.

'If the girl is really a princess,' the queen mused, *'she'll feel the hard pea and won't be able to sleep.'*

Well, sure enough, next morning the princess was exhausted.

'My dear, you look awful,' said the queen as they gathered at the breakfast table. *'Did you not sleep well?'*

'No, I didn't sleep at all last night,' said the princess, wearily. *'There was something hard in my bed, and I just couldn't get comfortable.'*

Uncomfortable

And that's like us. Who among us is ever totally comfortable in this fallen world, where we're not always treated with the love and respect, kindness and manners for which we were *created* as the Beloved Children of our God of Love?

Not me - I'm not comfortable with it! And neither is God, as His Word plainly reveals in every way, all the way to the Cross of Christ!

God created us to partake of His Sufficiency, His Watered Gardens of Divine Abundance, His Joy, His Peace, and to rejoice in the Ecstasy of His Divine Love, which is the only Love that can penetrate into our souls and satisfy us.

So it pains Him to see us trying to live happily in this fallen world on the meager rations of self-resources, self-defense, and mere human love. And to see us suffering the ill-effects of Satan's mind games and domination tactics.

And also to see us, three-part beings, trying to be happy and fulfilled on just two parts - our body and soul only - without Him in our spirit to complete us.

The Tender Heart of God

Truly, our Lord God feels very sorry for us. He is of infinite understanding, so He knows what we're suffering because of the Fall (Psalm 147:5; Isaiah 40:28; Luke 2:47).

Also, His Mercies are great, therefore His Heart goes out to us continually, calling each of us to return to Him by being born again with His Son's Life. He knows there is no real peace and rest when we're operating as our own god, when we're leaning on the arm of flesh - a broken reed at best.

He also knows the hidden fears that lurk within us when we have to rely on our own ingenuity and resources to save us from all the desolation, tragedy and badness in this world.

We may buck up every day, telling ourselves that we are strong, we can conquer the world, if we can think it, we can become it, 'I am woman, I am invincible.' But we were not made to have to buck up.

We were made to partake of the Sufficiency and Strength of *God Himself,* and to drink from the Everlasting Wells of *His* Joy, *His* Peace, *His* Abundance, *His* Power, and to be united in *Oneness* to *Him* - the One Who is so much Higher than us.

~ 20 ~

Cinderella's Shoe

'Oh, it's a perfect fit!'

BEFORE I met Jesus, I had no idea that I was living in the middle of the Fall of Man. Or that I was a Royal Daughter of the Most High.

No thanks to the Fall, Royal Amnesia regarding my True Identity had settled over my soul like a dense fog that had no edges and refused to roll.

Even so, I always felt a larger-than-life Identity within me. I would look at the trees and flowers, the sun, moon and stars, the oceans and mountains, and always I had a profound sense of Something Greater behind it all.

And I was stirred within by a feeling (an innate God-given knowledge, really) that I was more significant in the grand scheme of life than what appeared of me on the surface.

And I wasn't the only one feeling this way!. Over the years I've discovered that little girls everywhere were feeling that same significance within them.....and still do, generation after generation

A Greater Identity Within

Voltaire said, *"Life is absurd."* And I agree - with one caveat: Life in this *fallen* world is absurd. And no matter how Satan lies to us about who we are and where we came from, little girls innately know that that Greater Identity they feel within is more than a trinket not worth looking at.

They don't need an apparition or a ponderous knowledge of Greek and Latin, nor do they need thick books with grey covers to inform them of its existence. It strains for expression within them.

As it did within me as a child. I could feel a Greater Identity within me, held within the walls of my humanity. And although I could not put my finger on exactly what it was, I got a clue at an early age, when I was about six.

And like a dress designed and tailor-made for one's own personality and shape, this 'Greater Identity' felt right. No pinching, no tugging, just a perfect fit....like Cinderella's shoe. It was the identity of a princess.

Enchanting

I discovered this princess clue when my mother read the fairytales *Snow White* and *Sleeping Beauty* to me for the first time. I can still remember sitting beside her, gazing at the pictures, enthralled with the beauty and drama of each story. Such enchanting tales! Pretty princesses in beautiful dresses; sweet girls victimized by evil and then rescued by handsome princes on white horses.

I loved how dramatically the beautifully painted pictures in our family's over-sized, leather-bound storybook depicted the characters in each story. They showed how ugly the witch, how haughty and cruel the stepmothers.

They also showed how lovely and kind were the princesses, and I remember wondering why anyone, even a witch, would want to hurt them. It seemed akin to wanting to destroy flowers.

Something Beautiful Within

Between the two princesses, Snow White was my favorite. She was so sweet, even the birds weren't afraid to sit in her hand. I loved the adoring way they looked at her when she sang, so taken with her beauty and kindness.

Also, I loved how she brought great happiness into the lives of the seven dwarfs, turning their house into a real home and inspiring them to sing and laugh and dance.

Then my mother read the fairytale *Cinderella* to me. And I was instantly captivated by her ballgown! That dress with all its netting and sparkles practically made me shiver with desire. For not only was it beautiful, but it seemed to come with a promise. A promise that if I wore it, I would become like it - shimmering and beautiful.

141

And so, by the time my mother finished reading all three fairytales to me, my first dream for myself was fully formed, which was to *look* like and *be* like Snow White in Cinderella's ballgown.

'*If only I was all that,*' I dreamed, '*I would twirl and dance and make my gown sway and sparkle in the light. I would wear a tiara and wave my royal scepter, blessing everyone who came into my presence. We all would be so happy!*'

My first reality-check to this dream was that I couldn't sing like Snow White. When I tried, I croaked - like a nightingale with laryngitis.

And the birds wouldn't come near me either. Not one would sit on my proffered hand, even with seed in it.

Still, I knew there was *something* wonderful within me. '*If only I had that dress,*' I mused.

Like Mother, Like Daughter

My mother's childhood dreams must have been similar to mine, because sometime after she read the fairytales to me, she made pink chiffon dresses for my sister, Janet, and me.

And I was so excited! Now my princess dreams were going to come true, now I was going to have a princess dress!

And so, day after day, I watched as my dear mother laid out the chiffon material on our dining table, pinned the pattern pieces in place, and then cut the material.

And day after day, I watched as she skillfully sewed the fabric sections together, transforming herself into a Wondrous Weaver of dazzling dresses and Dispenser of stardust and little girls' dreams.

And when at last my dress was finished and she helped me into it, *finally,* I looked outwardly like I felt inwardly!

Then, to add the crowning touch, she placed a tiara on my head. Oh, it was really just a big pink bow she'd fashioned from the leftover material. *But it was a tiara to me!*

And with that, my fairytale dream became a reality: I was Snow White in Cinderella's ball gown! Now I could twirl, as at a princess ball.

And twirl I did! I twirled in front of the mirror, making my dress waft and swirl. I twirled in the yard, hoping the birds would bond with me. I twirled and danced like a ballerina, using a twig with an imaginary star on top to bless the universe with happiness.

And then one day, twirling in front of the mirror, it hit me: *I didn't look a thing like Snow White!* My hair was blond, not black like hers. And my dress was pink, not blue like Cinderella's. (Talk about buzz kill.)

Princesses from On High

But I wasn't the only one twirling and 'playing princess' back then. Little girls everywhere were doing the same - and still are.

For in some incomprehensible way, those beloved princess fairytales seem to speak to the depths of almost all little girls, saying,

'This is the real you - you are a Princess in disguise, and one day you'll *be restored to your rightful place in the Kingdom.'*

Little did I know back then that the reason little girls identify with being a princess is because they *are*!

We girls are the Royal Daughters of the Most High, created in the Image and Likeness of Heaven's Royalty. And I felt this Identity even as a child.

But I had Royal Amnesia. Like the rich young girl in the movie *Overboard* who lost her memory one night after falling off her yacht into the ocean.

Later, when she saw the 'sweaty carpenter' standing beside a dilapidated closet of old shoes, her memory jump-started a little, and she flashed back to her yacht's opulent shoe closet.

'The shoes!' she exclaimed. *'There's something about the shoes!'*

But that was as far as her memory could take her. It had given her a clue, pointing to her true identity, but she couldn't decipher it.

And neither could I decipher the 'Princess' clue within me, pointing to my own True Identity as one related to Heaven's Royalty.

Oh sure, I identified with being a princess. But with no evidence other than my feelings, I had to settle with *playing* princess. Like Faulkner's *Darl*, who imagined drinking the stars from a cedar water bucket while his family slept:

Well, after telling Mom this implausible story of mine, my dad sort of scratched his head and said to her, "You *know, I think that baby was pulling my leg!"* (That's an old colloquial expression meaning, *lying, tricking, hiding the truth.)*

Now, my sister, Pam, wasn't yet born when that happened. But once she was in this world, she grew into a beautiful woman blessed with a ton of wisdom from the Lord. And for many years she has said that, to her, "a lie never rings true…in fact, it doesn't ring at all!"

And neither did my lying little tale about how the Christmas tree fell. It just didn't ring true, either to my dad or my mom. She just laughed and said to him, *"Oh, Bill, it's obvious - Kathy tried to climb the Christmas tree!"*

The Ring of Our Royal Identity

I shared that little story with you just to say this: In the same way the truth rang in my mother's mind about me climbing the Christmas tree, I believe the Truth of our Royal Story portrayed in the fairytales *Snow White* and *Sleeping Beauty* rings in the hearts of most all little girls when they read them.

As to Cinderella, while she wasn't a princess, still little girls love how a handsome prince, after discovering her beauty and goodness, wooed her from her cinder ashes to become his royal bride.

Though her wicked stepmother had tried to keep her down, nevertheless, through a series of miraculous events, Cinderella was lifted to a status worthy of her goodness.

149

Heaven's Bell of Truth

Could it be that little girls identify with these princess fairytales because they hear Heaven's Bell of Truth ringing in their hearts about their own Princess Identity?

Could it be that they hear the melodious strains of their own Royal Heritage calling to them from deep within?

Can it be that before little girls learn to tie their own shoes, they already sense within themselves a Glorious Identity, clamoring to be found?

TRUTH

Part II

Our Royal Bridegroom

~ 22 ~

A Case for God

"Not by might, nor by power,
but by My Spirit, says the Lord of hosts."

(Zechariah 4:6)

CAN you imagine how much God didn't want us to die to Him? And how much it broke His Heart when we did?

Of course, some people might ask, '*Did God care when we died to Him in the Fall? Does He care now?*'

Natural questions, those. But they wouldn't really be fair. Because God tells us a thousand times in His Word that He does care, and that He loves us.

He says, *"I have loved you with an everlasting Love, therefore with loving-kindness have I drawn you"* (Jeremiah 31:3).

153

Beautiful! Yet still, some might answer, 'Yes, but has God forgotten our plight? Has He forgotten that we died to Him?'

No, never! God says, *"Can a woman forget her sucking child, that she should not have compassion on the child of her womb? They may forget, yet I will not forget you. Behold, I have engraved you on the Palms of My Hands: you are continually before Me"* (Isaiah 49:15-16).

Wonderful! So then the question remains: 'How can God fix our loss of both His Life in our spirit and His Nature in our soul without wiping us out and making another bunch that looks just like us?'

Seriously, our fallen nature is the polar opposite of God's Holy Nature. His goes one way, ours goes the other. Opposites are opposites, there's no way the two can be united in oneness together - at least not without one or both compromising or changing its nature.

That's a chemical and biological fact often demonstrated in our science labs: Although opposites attract, joining them together in intrinsic 'oneness' requires that the molecules of one or both are changed in some way.

And that's not going to happen with God! He plainly says, *"I change not"* (Malachi 3:6).

So What Are We to Do?

How then can we as fallen people get God back? Try to imitate Him in order to be like Him? Try to keep the Ten Commandments every day without fail? Exercise some religious protocol to try to make ourselves holy and unblameable in His Sight?

Well, good luck with that, because our fallen nature will sabotage those efforts, often sooner than later. God has shown us that fact very clearly in the Old Testament.

Besides, even if we *could* obey the Ten Commandments without fail, how would *that* fix our fallen nature's disposition? Really, how can 'good behavior' *change* our good and evil nature?

And even if it could, wouldn't our relationship to God be ever thereafter dependent on our good behavior? And wouldn't we always be in fear of blowing it and losing God again?

First John 4:18 says, *"There is no fear in love; perfect love casts out fear."*

Right. So then what's *God's* idea about how to fix our situation?

I mean, if we truly *are* His precious Children (which we are), fashioned in His Own Image and Likeness (which we were)......

......wouldn't it stand to reason that He would *never* stand idly by and let the devil trick us into losing our capacity to contain the Third and most vital Part of our beings (God's Life in our spirit) without doing anything about it?

My gosh, Snow White and Sleeping Beauty aren't even *real,* and they got raised from their sleeping death by princes on white horses.

Is it possible our Lord isn't any more of a hero than some fairytale prince charming?

Let's see about that - let's look at our own Prince Charming Story in the Bible. We've seen the first two correlations between our Royal Story and the fairytales *Snow White* and *Sleeping Beauty*.

Now let's see the third correlation, where just as they were raised from their sleeping death by true love, so are we!

~ 23 ~

The Villain, the Victim, and the Hero

*"Glory to God in the Highest,
and on Earth, peace, good will toward men."*

(Luke 2:14)

DOWN through the ages, our *real-life* Prince Charming Story has been called '*The Greatest Story Ever Told.*' And for good reason - revealed in it are the heights and depths of our Savior's Love for us!

We saw the tragic part of it back in Chapter 11, entitled 'A Short Synopsis of our Royal History.' But now let's look at it in its entirety and see *why* it has been called '*The Greatest Story Ever Told.*'

And not to be outdone by the drama and romance of *Snow White* and *Sleeping Beauty*, let's look at it in stage-play format, and call it: '*The Villain, the Victim, and the Hero.*'

157

~*The Villain, the Victim, and the Hero*~

Here is a syllabus of the cast, in order of hierarchy:

First, there's the Hero - Christ Jesus our Lord, the Second Person of the Trinity of God (Hebrews 1:1-3, 8 & 10), sometimes referred to herein as 'God' (denoting the entire Trinity).

Then there's the *Victim* - Mankind (collectively representing Adam, Eve, you, me, *all* people); also referred to herein as 'the Beloved Princess' and 'God's Beloved.'

Lastly, there's the *Villain* – Satan the devil, that evil fallen angel who......well, we all know who *he* is.

So let's begin:

ACT I

The curtain opens on our Prince Charming Story with God's Beloved going about Her innocent way in the Garden of Eden.

In the background is the Villain, making his way to approach her, having finalized his plot to take over the Earth and make Her his subject.

Burning with hatred for Her because She is God's Beloved, and also because God had made Her in His own Image, and had given Her dominion over the Earth (Genesis 1:26), the Villain has hatched a sinister plan, one designed to do three things:

1) separate Her from God

2) thereby gain spiritual dominion over Her and the Earth

3) subject Her ever thereafter to his torments

Why does the Villain want to torment Her?

Because the only pleasure he gets is in causing pain and suffering to others – the result of trying to destroy the God of Love and take over His Throne in Heaven.

And the Villain knows just how to accomplish his cruel purposes!

Lie to God's Beloved! And lie in such a tricky way that She'll be enticed into eating the fruit of the forbidden tree, which will change Her nature!

Full well the Villain knows that because She has never before heard a lie, chances are She won't detect his deceptions.

And so he sidles up to Her, feigning the persona of something good and wise, and says, '*Has God said you can eat of all the trees of the Garden?*'

She replies, '*We may eat of all the trees, except for the Tree of the Knowledge of Good and Evil; for God says that in the day we eat of it, we shall die.*'

'You shall not die!' the Villain lies. *'For God knows that in the day you eat of it, you shall be as God, knowing good and evil!'*

There, the Villain not only blatantly refutes God's Word and basically calls Him a liar; but he insinuates that the reason God didn't want the Beloved to eat the forbidden fruit was because God was trying to keep Her from being all She could be.

How ironic, how ludicrous! Here's the Villain, *"a liar and the father of lies"* (as Jesus said of him in John 8:44), wickedly accusing the *God of Truth* of being a liar!

But sadly, the deception works. God's Beloved Princess *believes* the Villain. And having unwittingly swallowed the Villain's lies, now She swallows the forbidden fruit.

Apparently, it never occurred to Her that what the Villain said about God wasn't true. Granted, She didn't know such a thing as a lie even existed, so in that respect She truly is a Victim of the Villain's deception (Romans 7:11; First Timothy 2:14; Revelation 12:9).

On the other hand, She's a red-handed rebel against God! Because not only had God told Her that She would die if She ate the good and evil fruit, but He had *commanded* Her not to eat it!

But She eats it anyway. And dies to God.

ACT II

Destitute of God's Presence now, and lost to Eternal Life with Him, the Beloved Princess - a three-part being - now finds Herself operating on only two-parts, in a world where sin and evil now exist and bad things will happen to....um, not-so-good-now-people.

And the Villain is ecstatic! His wicked plan worked! God's Beloved has been tricked into receiving part of his evil nature. And by his trickery, She has unwittingly given him spiritually legal ground to influence Her behavior through the evil part of Her now good and evil nature!

Gleefully, he celebrates, tantalized by the prospect of victimizing Her throughout the ages to come.

ACT III

A death pall looms over the Garden of Eden now. The Beloved of God has died to Him. Her Beautiful Birthplace has now become Her grave.

Sorrowfully, God calls to Her: *'Where are you? What have you done?'* (Genesis 3:9).

Full well He knows where She is and what She's done, but He is distracted in His grief.

All Heaven grieves with Him. And the Villain snickers in the background.

ACT IV

Silence prevails on our stage now. The end has come, the tragedy done. Turn out the lights, Maestro, our Story is over.

Slowly, sadly, the curtain begins to close.....

* * *

But wait, what's that sound? Do you hear it? I hear it - sounds like horse hooves to me! Open that curtain, Maestro......

Ah yes, I see......it *is* a horse - a *white* horse (Revelation 19:11)! And riding on it is Someone the Villain has yet to reckon with! *The Hero - the King of kings and Lord of lords! His Royal Majesty* is coming, for He too has a Plan!

Which is this: While He is here on Earth, He will let the Villain influence the people to hang Him on a Cross. There, He will take all the Victim's sins - past, present and future - into His own sinless Body, so that when He dies, all Her sins will die with Him!

Then, after three days, He will rise to New Life and leave all Her sins behind Him, dead and buried in His Grave forever!

And the Hero carries out His Plan to perfection! He takes all Her sins into His Holy Body on the Cross and with Him to His Grave!

Then He rises from the dead to New Life, leaving Her sins behind, dead and buried forever.

He had Power to lay down His Life, and He has Power to take it again, as He told the people in advance of His Crucifixion, saying:

> *"I lay down my Life, that I may take it again: no man takes it from Me, but I lay it down of Myself. I have*

162

Power to lay it down, and I have Power to take it again.
This I have received of My Father."

(John 10: 17-18)

The Victim had been suffering separation from God through Her indwelling sin nature. But now the Hero has paid the price for all Her sins – past, present, and future – so that She could be set free from the power and condemnation of sin, as well as from the power and authority of the Villain.

"For as much as the Children [of God] were partakers
of flesh and blood, so Jesus also took part of the same,
that through death He might destroy him who had the
power of death - that is, the devil - and deliver them..."

(Hebrews 2:14-15)

And now the Hero calls to Her, saying:

"Awake, thou that sleepest! Rise from the dead [from
your death to God sleep of the Fall of Man], and Christ
shall give you Light [the Light of the Life of the Trinity
of God, resulting in Eternal Life]."

(Ephesians 5:14)

And She hears Him! From the depths of Her death-sleep, She stirs at His Voice of Love and opens Her heart to Him and receives His Divine Life!

163

"....and [She] that hears the Voice of the Son of God shall live.
For as God the Father has Life in Himself,
so He has given God the Son to have Life in Himself."

(John 5:25-26)

"And through Christ we receive, not the spirit of the world,
but the Spirit which is of God."

(First Corinthians 2:12)

With the Hero's Life now dwelling in Her soul, it's as if *She Herself* had paid the full price for Her sins!

For in *God's Judgment*, all Her sins were buried with Him, qualifying Her to be raised to New Life with Jesus when She receives His Divine Life into Her soul and spirit!

"For God, Who is rich in Mercy, for His great Love wherewith He loved us,

even when we were dead in sins, has quickened us together with Christ (for by Grace are you saved),

and has raised us up and made us sit together in Heavenly Places in Christ."

(Ephesians 2:4-6)

"And now you are complete in Him [Jesus] Who is the Head of all principality and power....

*buried with Him in [His] death...and raised to New
Life with Him through faith [in what He did for you on
the Cross]."*

(Colossians 2:10, 12)

**And with that, the wicked plan of the Villain is defeated, once
and for all!**

* * *

And there you have it, dearly Beloved of God – there is our own
Prince Charming Story!

But ours is no fairytale! In real time and real history, Jesus carried
out His Plan to accomplish our Salvation, and then He sat down at the
Right Hand of the Majesty On High!

*Jesus – "the Brightness of God's Glory,
and the Express Image of His Person...*

*when He had by Himself purged our sins, sat
down at the Right Hand of the Majesty on High..."*

(Hebrews 1:3)

Oh, what a magnificent scene *that* must have been! Christ Jesus,
the King of kings and Lord of lords, triumphantly entering the Holy
of Holies in Heaven and sitting down at the Right Hand of God the

Father, having destroyed once and for all the curse of sin and the power and authority of Satan over our souls!

Want a real He-Man, Sister? One who'll go out there in the universe and fight off your tormentors without giving up or running home cryin' to his mama?

Look at how the KING OF KINGS fought to the death for you! Behold how He gave Himself to be tortured to save you (and all of us) without so much as a whimper!

See how He rose from the dead and sat down at the Right Hand of God the Father without seeking a shred of sympathy!

You know, I always thought it so romantic how Snow White and Sleeping Beauty's prince charmings awakened them with a kiss. But when I met Jesus, I realized that, hey, it cost our Prince Charming more than just a kiss to awaken us from our sleeping death - it cost Him His Life!

Through great pain and torment, He gave His earthly Life that we might have His Eternal Life.

He wore an earthly crown of thorns on the Cross so that we could be Crowned with His Divine Life (Second Timothy 4:7-8).

He rose from the dead so that we could rise from our sleeping death to God and "sit together with Him in Heavenly Places" as His Bride (John 3:29; Ephesians 2:5-6).

And when we do rise by receiving His Life, then we are Crowned by God as 'THE ROYAL BRIDE OF THE KING OF KINGS AND LORD OF LORDS,' even while we are still here in this world!

And that makes us the Head and not the tail in relation to the Villain!

Now, that's what the Bible calls *Grace*......and *Mercy!* Grace and Mercy that are each greater than all our sin (Zachariah 4:7; Matthew 9:13; John 1:17; Romans 3:21-28; Galatians 2:21)!

Little wonder on the night Jesus was born, a company of angels came to the shepherds, singing, "Peace on Earth, goodwill toward men!" As my sister, Pam, describes it:

"The King of kings and Lord of lords left His Throne on High to come to our rescue. Heaven opened its Royal Doors to let His Majesty pass through. Supernovas moved aside for Him. Constellations placed a Star over His Manger. Angels and wise men worshipped Him......and the devil trembled!"

~ *24* ~

Love as Strong as Death

"Set Me as a seal upon your heart, upon your arm,
for My Love for you is as strong as death."

(Song of Solomon 8:6)

I BET the devil tore his hair out on the Day of Pentecost! That Glorious Day Jesus sent down His Divine Life from Heaven to live within us (Acts 2:1-4)! (That's probably why Darth Vader wears a hoodie.)

I can just imagine the shock on Satan's evil face when he realized that Jesus had turned His horrific sufferings on the Cross into a Gift of His Life to live within us (Ephesians 2:22)!

No doubt Satan thought he'd secured his eternal victory over us when Jesus died - but he had another think coming! The Lord blindsided him with His Cross, *big time!*

169

For not only did Jesus break Satan's power of eternal death over us through His Cross and Resurrection, but when we are born again, Satan's spiritual authority over us is broken as well! Because now Jesus dwells within us, *and Satan has no power or authority over Jesus!*

Oh, how this must have irked Satan's evil pride when he realized *why* Jesus had submitted Himself to the Cross! Well, you know what the Bible says: *"Pride goes before destruction and a haughty spirit before a fall"* (Proverbs 16:18).

And *nobody* has more pride than Satan! It was his pride that motivated him as an angel in Heaven to try to take over God's Throne - but he was cast out (Isaiah 14:12-15).

It was his pride that made him believe that he would always have authority and power over Mankind (Hebrews 2:14) - and yet he lost it through Jesus' Cross and Resurrection.

And it's Satan's narcissistic, egotistical pride and selfish lust for power and worship that motivates him today to blind people to Salvation through Jesus (Second Corinthians 4:4).

And yet Satan is foiled again and again, as generation after generations of people hear about Jesus and are born again!

The Name that is Above Every Name

Truth is, if anyone has a right to be filled with pride, it's *Jesus,* not the devil! Jesus is the KING OF KINGS AND LORD OF LORDS of the universe (Revelation 19:6)!

And yet with all that, He *never* pridefully elevates Himself over us! This is what the Bible tells us about Him, and this is the experience of untold billions of people who have known Him down through the centuries.

Countless songs and books and poems have been written about Him by Believers with experiential knowledge of Him, all attesting to His immense Love and Faithfulness in lifting their souls into the Presence of God and showering them with His Favor and Blessings.

And many also attest to Jesus' Majesty and Power in setting them free from bondage to Satan and demons – evil spirits they didn't even know they were dominated by until they met Jesus.

Truly, Jesus is an amazing dichotomy - He is *El Elyon* - "the Lord Most High" (Genesis 14:19) - and yet He *never* makes us feel like He is looking down on us!

I must say, though, being treated so magnanimously by Someone Who is *all that,* is actually quite shocking (at least it has been to me!). But we can understand it better when we think of a dear, loving mother: Would she ever lord herself over her children, as if she's just so-o-o much better than them? Of course not!

Oh, maybe a mother gripped by the power of the enemy might do that (pride being a trait of the devil and all).

But no other mother *ever* elevates herself arrogantly above her children. Instead, she tries to elevate them and give them every advantage so that they can reign in life. And when she can't do all that, it breaks her heart.

So it is with Jesus and our Heavenly Father and the Holy Spirit! We were created in Their Image and Likeness to be the Head and not the tail in life here on Earth (Genesis 1:26-27).

God meant us to reign victoriously and joyfully as dear Sons and Daughters, endowed with all the rights, privileges and honor afforded the Family of Heaven's Royalty. And when we lost it all through the Fall, Jesus went forth in great Power to restore it to us by giving us His Life!

Oh, dear friend, never was a woman so loved by a man, never a child by a parent, never a friend by a friend, as we are loved by our Savior! Never has the world seen such Love than the day Jesus climbed the hill of Calvary to break Satan's power of death and dominion over us!

And now, combining the prophecy of Jesus in Isaiah 42:13 with Jesus' Words in Luke 23:34, we see His Love for us and His Passion for the Salvation of our souls foretold and fulfilled:

"The Lord shall go forth as a Mighty Man,
He shall stir up [His] jealousy [for us] like a Man of War:
He shall cry, yes, roar [when being crucified by the people, saying],

'FATHER, FORGIVE THEM,
FOR THEY KNOW NOT WHAT THEY DO.'

And He shall prevail against His enemies
[Satan and the Fall of Man]."

172

~ 25 ~

Onward and Upward

"...Come, let us go up to the mountain of the Lord....
He will teach us His ways, and we will walk in His paths..."

(Isaiah 2:3)

THE Bible says that when we are born again by putting on the Royal Clothing of Jesus' Life, we are ***"born***, *not of [earthly] blood, nor of the will of the flesh, nor of the will of man, but **of God**"* (John 1:13).

Honestly though, I'd never even heard the term "born again" until I met Jesus and it happened to me. And to say the least, it was the most *wonderful, life-changing, ecstatically joyful experience I NEVER could have dreamed of!*

And now it pleases the Lord that I tell you all about it - what caused me to desire to know Him, what finally drew me to Him, and how I met Him.

But where to start? *"How is it possible to bring order out of memory?"* wrote one of the first women pilots about growing up in Africa:

> *"I should like to start at the beginning, patiently, like a weaver at his loom. I should like to say, This is the place to start; there can be no other.*
>
> *But there are a hundred places to start...and I am no weaver. Weavers create. This is remembrance, re-visitation, corridors no longer fresh in the mind, yet nonetheless familiar in the heart."*

We all have "corridors of remembrance" no longer fresh in our minds, don't we!? Yet the circumstances that led me to Jesus and how I met Him are *ever familiar* to me, both in my mind and my heart. And it will be my privilege to show Him to you from the heights of my own life's mountaintop.

We'll have to start out in the valley, though. For as all mountain roads wind along the valley floor before they climb higher and higher to where the air becomes exquisite and the panorama below spreads itself beyond the horizon, and one feels like a little ant reaching out to greater things for itself, so my life's road goofed around on the valley floor awhile before it turned sharply and made a steep ascent to God.

Climbing

Personally, I think that anyone who has spiritually climbed 'God's Mountain' (metaphorically spoken of in Psalm 48:1), and then looked back to write about their life in the valley, secretly considers the possibility that they might end up writing a microscopic epic of human absurdity and then flinging it out there for all the world to gasp and laugh at (to borrow a phrase from one funny guy in a writer's magazine).

But hey, I've been laughed at before! Like the time I was enjoying lunch with my husband and our (then) little children at the zoo one afternoon:

When I stood up from the picnic table to go get a soda at the concession stand, the little hairpiece I was wearing on top of my long hair caught on the table's umbrella, and I walked off without it.

Hearing a sudden burst of laughter behind me, I turned around to see what was so funny, and there was my family, laughing and pointing at my hairpiece hanging like laundry on a line, dangling in the breeze without me.

Life's.....a Bowl of Cherries?

Back in the 60's, Erma Bombeck wrote a book entitled, *If Life's a Bowl of Cherries, Why Am I in the Pits?* And hmm, I wonder: Did she too get her hairpiece caught on a line?

If so, did she too toss it into the air several times before slam-dunking it into the nearest trashcan, secretly vowing to never wear that stupid thing again?

And when she officially entered her 'golden years, ' did she, like me, understand that it's hard to hold a pose and look elegant 24/7? And that even if you can, it's boring anyway?

And that just when you're at your finest, there's always some quirky circumstance waiting just around the corner to turn the water hose on you, just to help you keep things in perspective?

Well, I don't know what Erma's conclusions were in her golden years, but here's mine: When we give our hearts to Jesus and receive His Life, He invites us to enjoy the cherries and trust Him with the pits. Just bank every situation on His Goodness and Mercy.

Because as the One Who loves us eons beyond what we can imagine, in spite of our faults, Jesus delights in delivering us from all evil (in whatever form it comes) and bringing good into our lives. That's just Who He is!

And He loves to show us that He is *the Lord of Love* Who will *never* fail to deliver us, whether the negatives in our lives are our own fault or not! And that's what you'll see in my life, not only in this volume, but in those to come.

Also, you'll see that it was not just the positives but the negatives of life that influenced me to turn against the emptiness and lies of the world, the flesh, and the devil, and instead embrace our Lord of Love.

And when I did, to my great delight I discovered that I had joined up with the coolest Chicks on the planet - *Chicks for Jesus*!

~ 26 ~

Mirror, Mirror, On the Wall

"She stood in the Hall of a Thousand Mirrors..."

LOOKING back on what led me to become a Chick for Jesus, I realize it all began when I was a child, feeling a Greater Identity within me than I could express. And the only role models that spoke to this feeling were the princess identities of Snow White and Sleeping Beauty, as I shared with you earlier.

Later on, when I turned twelve, something shifted within me (hello puberty), and this 'Greater Identity' clamored for expression, and without even realizing what I was doing, I set out to express *myself,* make *myself* happy, find *my* place in the world.

And I was thrilled with myself! I could see in the mirror how quickly I was changing from a child into a young lady, and it was like watching a small miracle unfold:

My face began to mature, my scrawny torso began to fill out (sort of), and with my dishwater-blond hair, I began to look more and more like Sleeping Beauty with every passing day.

Too bad, because with her blond hair and light skin, I always thought she looked sort of pale and frail. Not at all exotic-looking like Snow White (my favorite among the princesses).

Oh well, we all have to go with what we've got, right? So I decided to focus on Sleeping Beauty's good points. After all, there was *one* prince in her story who thought she was fantastic; maybe there would be one in mine!

A Romantic Viewpoint

Twelve was a weird age - too old to be a child, too young to be a woman. On one hand, I still had the remnants of a child's imagination, and on the other, I had an increasing comprehension of grown-up love and romance.

And when these morphed together, some very interesting scenes came forth! Like the one I imagined one night laying on my bed, pretending that Snow White and Sleeping Beauty's death plight was now my own:

I was eternally asleep, lying on my cushy, flower-strewn bed, with the boy down the street (on whom I had a crush) standing beside me, in love and stricken with grief that he didn't have the power of a true prince in his kiss to awaken me from my curse-induced slumber and make me his bride.

178

Oh, how romantic it was, lying there, basking in his adoring gaze (while trying hard to look serene and lovely and not blink). Oh, how beautiful I was!

Then, with nowhere else to go with that scene, and no way to respond to him (because, after all, I *was* supposed to be *dead*), I imagined that he turned to my mother (who was suddenly standing nearby) to express his grief that I would never be his.

He....turned....to....my....*mother.* Can you imagine? My *mommy* is in the most romantic scene of my life!

And she *consoles* him! The two of them are *bonding* while I lay there lost to the world!

But hey, I loved the whole episode anyway, and replayed it from start to finish again and again that night. Until I got bored with it (ya think?) and fell asleep.

I don't remember reenacting that scene any time after that night, though. Not because I didn't love it, but because soon thereafter, the 'chick' *nom de plume* came into vogue, and I discovered the possibility of being a real live 'princess chick' – one who was up and around and expressing her princess identity instead of sleeping it off.

~ 27 ~

Cool Chicks, Hip Chicks, Everything-in-Between-Chicks

'If you aren't one, fake it.'

BY the time I was in high school, the 'chick' term had expanded into *types* of chicks. Not only were there chicks and cute chicks, but a plethora of other kinds of chicks as well.

There were cool chicks, hip chicks, athletic chicks, hodad chicks (girls whose boyfriends rode motorcycles and wore black leathers to school), funny chicks, book-worm chicks, and everything-in-between-chicks.

As for me, I wouldn't have dared tell anyone that I identified with being a 'princess chick' (lest I be called childish by my peers), so I kept it to myself.

But then one day I saw some 'surfer chicks' walking down the hallway at school, looking the epitome of what I imagined 'cool chicks' should look like.

They were tan, had the sun-streaked-hair look of those who spent a lot of time in the sun, and they walked with a cool, calm demeanor that none of the rest of the girls seemed to have. So I decided to become one of them.

The Illuminati of the Sea

My first order of transformation was to acquire a Pendleton. This was a light-weight wool plaid shirt that surfers wore unbuttoned over their shirts or blouses year 'round.

Considered essential surfer fashion back then, a Pendleton was the one piece of clothing that identified you as a surfer. So I got myself a yellow and blue-plaid Pendleton and wore it to school every day.

My dishwater-blond hair was already a little sun-streaked from my frequent trips to the beach, so to that I added a slower walk, a calmer demeanor, as if I too were part of the Illuminati of the Sea.

Oh, I can't tell you how groovy I felt, walking around campus, pretending to be a surfer. That is, until someone asked me what it was like to catch a wave, and why I didn't have a tan.

Then I knew - it was either get a tan and learn to surf, or ditch the Pendleton.

Off to the Beach

Learning to surf wasn't easy. On the first day out, I got a sunburn....*and* an earache from the waves pounding into my ears and up my nose. On cold days I shivered in the water until my teeth chattered and my lips turned blue.

Other days my eyes turned fiery red from having salt water blasted into them because I couldn't get my (borrowed) surfboard turned around fast enough.

Then one day I actually caught a wave....or rather, *it caught me.* I was way out past the breakers, paddling back in, when suddenly a huge wall of water rose from under me, hauled me up to its crest and then drove me at breakneck speed toward shore.

And wow! That's all I can say, just *wow!* White knuckling it on top of an uncontrollable wall of water racing toward shore, even while it held me up as gracefully as an English duchess holds a teacup, was amazing fun! Exhilarating!

Then, just as daintily as that same duchess might return her teacup to its saucer, the spent wave deposited me gently onto the sand and rushed back out to sea to pick up another hopeful traveler.

And lying there on my surfboard, eye to eye with the sand and seaweed, my heart racing with adrenaline, I understood why the surfer chicks always looked so serene and happy.

183

~ 28 ~

Wanna' be a Beatnik Chick

"Far out, man."

A CLOUD of cigarette smoke hovered in a corner of the lowly-lit San Francisco coffee house. There, perched on a wooden chair atop a low makeshift stage, a Beatnik dressed in black was calmly reciting his poetry to a small audience of other Beatniks sitting in front of the stage.

The group, seven or eight of them, listened pensively to the recitation, some gazing thoughtfully into the distance, others checking out the ceiling, or looking down at the floor as if seeing something profound in the wooden planks.

When the poetry reading was over, I heard a faint murmur of *"Far out, man"* as the reader stepped down from the stage and another guy ascended to read his prose.

This was my first experience of Beatniks. I was fifteen at the time, and I had been in the San Francisco area for a week or so visiting relatives when a cousin invited me to go cruising with her on Saturday night.

Naturally, I accepted her invitation. Joyriding with my 'older' cousin (she was all of sixteen) in her car on a Saturday night seemed like great fun, no matter where we went or what we did!

But I needed to go clothes shopping first. Hailing from the Southern California beach area as I did, I'd made the mistake of assuming that there would be surfer girls everywhere in and around San Francisco, and that my Pendleton and surfer sandals would fit right in.

But when I arrived at the airport and got off the plane, there wasn't a surfer in sight. None in the terminal, none on the streets, none anywhere. Just me. And I was a poser.

So I went shopping and bought a sweater to replace my Pendleton, and a pair of silver flats to replace my sandals.

Out on the Town

When Saturday night *finally* rolled around, my cousin and I went joyriding in The City (as the locals call San Francisco).

Then she took me to the coffeehouse where the Beatniks were hanging out. And I loved the place the moment we walked in!

The atmosphere was cozy and inviting, lit softly to simulate candlelight, and the two large wood-paneled rooms were crowded with young people.

Adding to the ambiance, contemporary music played softly through the sound system, and the aroma of brewed coffee and freshly baked pastries sweetened the air.

My cousin, having been there many times, swiftly navigated our way to an empty table in a corner of one of the rooms, right next to the Beatniks. And after a waitress came and took our order, we began chatting about our lives.

And that's when I slowly became aware of the Beatniks and what was happening over in their corner. Most of them were dressed in black – black pants, black turtlenecks, black t-shirts.

And seeing that there was some sort of reading going on, I assumed they were a book club or a writing group, and I asked my cousin about them.

"They're Beatniks," she said.

Well, I'd never heard of Beatniks. So she explained that they are 'existentialists' – people who think deeply into their existence and write down their thoughts, usually in the form of poetry or prose, and then they gather to read their writings to one another - *"like they're doing now,"* she said.

About this time, one of her classmates stopped by our table to say 'hi,' and after she introduced me to him and they began chatting, I

187

took the opportunity to shift inconspicuously in my chair a little, so I could listen in on the Beatniks. I found the subject of 'existentialism' fascinating, and I wanted to know what they were saying about it.

Eavesdropping

Without turning my face totally in their direction, I listened with one ear, trying to discern what they were saying above the music and the din of the crowd. But all I could hear were catchphrases like, *'Far out, man'* and *'Really cool, dude.'*

Then, as one Beatnik was leaving the stage after his reading, I heard one of the guys in the group say to him, *'Really heavy, man.'*

And in my mind, I was like, *'What's really heavy? Talk louder man, I can't heeeaarr you!'*

But the Beatniks were just too laid back, talked too softly, and I knew I was never going to hear what they were saying.

So I decided to think deeply into my own life. *'Hey, I have a life,'* I told myself. *'I'm not totally devoid of something to write about.'*

And with that, I stared down at the floor and tried to think deeply about my own existence. You know, like, get really heavy into it.

But all I remember getting 'really heavy into' that night was how cool my new shoes were.

~ 29 ~

Hippie Chicks

"Flower children"

AS I recall, the 'chick' term hit the scene simultaneously with the birth of rock and roll, in the late 1950's. We now call those first rock songs 'Oldies but Goodies,' but back then they made a new sound.

It was a fun sound, but with its heavy emphasis on the drums, most older people found it quite primitive and sort of shocking.

But I loved it! As enthralled as I was with classical music – Bach, Beethoven, Chopin, Brahms - still, I loved the invigorating sound of rock and roll, as did most of America's youth.

I also loved the dance steps that came with the first rock song - *'Rock around the Clock.'* It was a tricky little back-and-forth shuffle with one foot, while doing a heel-toe-heel-toe step with the other, which was really fun, even for the adults that tried it.

Then came Bobbie Day singing *'Rockin' Robin.'* Soon Elvis Presley topped the charts, and Chubby Checker sang *'The Twist,'* setting Americans to twisting and turning until their hips practically dislocated.

Then more songs came, introducing more dances, like *The Boogaloo*, *The Pony*, *The Watusi*, and *The Skate*, to name a few.

By 1964, the Beatles were famous, and as their music evolved and their hair grew long, young people everywhere followed their example. And with that, the counterculture of the Hippie Era was ushered in, which hit the scene so fast, even I hadn't seen it coming.

In fact, the first time I learned of it was at a rock concert in Hollywood one night. And I was so impressed by the whole experience, that years later I wrote a little novella about it.

It begins: *The first time I stepped onto Hollywood's Sunset Boulevard, I was nineteen and looking for adventure.....*

> *In our purses, my friend, Alice, and I had tickets to a rock concert that seemed more like tickets to paradise than to a fleeting night of music.*
>
> *We joy rode into Hollywood in my little corvette convertible, our hair blowing in the wind, us singing along with the music blasting from the radio, my croaky voice floating like bubbles into the midnight blue, where the stars seemed to be twinkling with laughter at it like kids at a slumber party.*

CHICKS FOR JESUS

Anyway, when we arrived in Hollywood and stepped onto Sunset Boulevard ('the Strip,' as the locals call it), we were thrilled to see the Saturday night scene in full swing.

People as colorful as unsorted beads dotted the sidewalks, their faces and fashions illumined by the bright neon signs atop the boulevard's establishments.

On the street, sleek new automobiles showed off their elegantly dressed passengers, while tricked-out old cars cruised by slowly, rumbling their engines and blaring their music.

The year was 1966. And standing there on Sunset Boulevard with my friend, we were both ready to dance the night away to the music of one of our favorite rock bands.

Let's go, we tacitly agreed when the light turned green. We crossed the street to the other side of the boulevard and began the short, one-block trek to the club where the concert was being held.

Oh, I can't tell you what a cool chick I felt like: the bell-bottoms of my hip-hugger jeans flipping back and forth over my shoes as we walked; the hanging beads of my crop-top swaying rhythmically with each step; my long ponytail swishing from side to side.

The Glitterati of Groove

A throng of young people were milling about under the bright lights of the club's marquee when we arrived, waiting for the doors to open. Many looked to be our age – in their late teens.

191

Which normally would have posed a problem since the age requirement for admittance to a nightclub in California is 21. But this was one of those special nights when the club closed its liquor bar and dropped the age requirement to eighteen.

As expected, young people arrived like sojourning acolytes, ready to groove to the music of one of their favorite bands. And we were among them. We were all young, energetic, and ready to rock 'n roll.

While waiting for the doors to open, my friend and I stood shyly on the sidewalk, somewhat intimidated by all the cool, hip-looking people gathered in one place. To me, they were like the 'Beautiful People' I'd heard about – the In-Crowd, the Glitterati of Groove.

And I felt like a closet rubbernecker checking out their fashions and hairstyles as nonchalantly as I could.

But soon I noticed some of them checking *us* out, like maybe they thought *we* were part of the 'Beautiful People' too. And man, did I feel like a cool, hip chick then!

That is, until *they* arrived. Two girls and a guy. And then all my ideas about what was hip and cool flew out the proverbial window.

Hippie Chicks

The girls wore sandals, long skirts, and white linen blouses with lots of delicately beaded necklaces. One girl had dark wavy hair crowned with a wreath of tiny white flowers.

child. I didn't remember it at the time of my encounter with her, but years later I would learn of it from a friend.

This friend and I had often played together when we were children, as our families were close. Later, when we grew up and lived hundreds of miles apart, we stayed in touch through occasional phone calls and visits.

Well, one day, about fifteen years after my encounter with that Hippie Chick, this friend phoned me and said that she was in town and would like to drop by for a visit.

I said something like, 'Come on down,' and when she arrived, we sat in my family room and drank iced tea and caught up on news. But not too long into our visit, her eyes began to tear up, and she said she had something to tell me.

I couldn't imagine what it was. Did she have a fatal disease? Had one of her children become seriously ill? Was she getting a divorce?

Nope, none of the above. Instead, she slowly, painfully told me a story that involved the two of us when we were very young.

She said that when she was about six, and I was about two and a half, my mom was babysitting her one day at my house. And as we were playing together in the backyard, she said to me, *'Kathy, get into your wagon and I'll take you for a ride.'*

So I climbed in, and off we went down the street. But instead of turning around after a couple of blocks and taking me home, she parked me in a covert of tall bushes and told me terrible things about myself; including that I was a horrible person and that nobody loved me, especially my mom and dad, and that they didn't want me anymore.

Then she said, *'Don't try to go home! Nobody wants you!'* And with that, she left me there in the bushes and ran back to my yard to play.

Mum's the Word

Well, eventually my mom looked out the kitchen window, and seeing her in the yard but not me, she called out, *'Where's Kathy?'*

And my friend called back and said, *'Oh, she's just behind the chicken coop. I'll go get her and bring her into the house.'*

Then she ran down the street to fetch me.

Rushing into the bushes, she found me sitting in the red wagon (probably all red-eyed and puffy-faced from crying). And desperate to console me so that I wouldn't tell on her, she quickly explained that she had lied, that my parents really did love me, and that she was taking me home.

Then she told me to quit crying and not tell my parents or anyone what had happened. And I never did. In fact, I must have blocked the incident out of my mind early on, because all my life I didn't even remember it.

But the damage was done. The traumatic message now grooved onto my impressionable child-brain was that I was such a horrible person, nobody could or ever would love me.

Believing the Lie

Fast-forwarding many years later, to the day this friend came to my house and tearfully recounted this incident to me, although I didn't remember it, I *did* remember how she had treated me throughout our growing up years.

I remembered how she would roll her eyes at me when I talked, as if what I was saying was stupid. And I remembered how she would laugh and make fun of me, even ridicule me at times - all behind our parents' backs so they couldn't see or hear what she was saying and doing.

And I also remembered how I'd never held any of it against her. I had always known that her childhood was hard; I had been aware of it even as a little girl.

And now, sitting with her in my home, seeing her tears and hearing how sorry she was, I felt deep compassion for her.

So I told her not to worry about it, that it was no big deal, that I didn't remember that red wagon incident anyway. Then I hugged her and assured her that I forgave her and that I still loved her.

Pondering

After she left my house that day, however, I pondered on this 'red wagon' experience I'd gone through, and I realized that I had probably blocked it out of my mind early on because it was so traumatic.

Then I pondered on another incident, a beautiful one that had taken place a couple of years after that red wagon debacle, when I was about five.

And not only had I *never* forgotten it, I'd always cherished the memory of it. And thinking of it that day, after my friend left my house, I realized something profound:

That is, that God, *Jehovah El-Roi* – 'the God Who Sees' – had seen me sitting alone in my red wagon after my friend ditched me, perhaps looking up into the sky through my tears and wondering if there was anyone 'Up There' who loved me, anyone who might want me as their very own child.

And He had answered me.

He had seen my little friend groove that hurtful message onto my still-forming child mind, one saying that I was so horrible that nobody loved me, or ever would.

And so a few years later, when I was five, He grooved His own Message onto my heart and mind......

~ 31 ~

Blue Skies and Butterflies

"O satisfy us early with Your mercy [dear God],
that we may rejoice [in Your Love]....
For I am poor and needy, and my
heart is wounded within me."

(Psalm 90.14; 109:22)

IT'S been said of Jesus, *"The King always has one more move."* And that saying came true in my life when God checkmated that traumatic red wagon message that had not only pierced my heart but had been imprinted on my physical brain.

And He did it just a few short years after that incident, as my mother was walking me home from school one afternoon.

It was just a short walk, only three blocks. But to me, a wide-eyed kindergartener, it was always a great adventure when my mom arrived at school on foot, instead of picking me up in the car.

201

I loved walking by the little corner market where an old ice cream cooler hummed just inside the screen door, and jars of brightly colored candy stood delectably on the counter.

And I loved how the sweet aroma of chocolate bars, peanut taffy, fruity bubble gum, and other candies mingled sweetly together and wafted out to the sidewalk, drawing us in for an occasional treat.

Also, I loved turning the corner from the little market and seeing the tall, majestic trees that lined our street. They seemed a stately regiment, set to guard us from the heat of the day by casting their cool ponds of shade over the sidewalk.

Even now I can hear the delightful rustling sound their heart-shaped leaves made whenever a breeze passed through them, like thousands of tiny children clapping their hands with joy.

And Then There Was Love

It was under the shade of those stately trees that day, while walking home with my mother, that God grooved His own Message onto my heart and mind.

I can still picture how fresh everything looked, as if a gentle shower of rain had passed by the night before and washed the dust off everyone's faces.

The flowers and foliage sparkled, and overhead, tall stacks of billowing clouds glistened in the sun, as if Someone had adorned them with robes of light and sent them to play in the wide-open spaces.

And as it happened, as my mom and I were nearing home, walking hand in hand in companionable silence, a sparkle of light from one of those stately trees caught my eye.

And I looked up just in time to see a bright light shoot down and cover everything over with such Love that, instantly, I was filled with happiness!

Love like I had never dreamed existed, indescribably Higher and Purer and Bigger than mere earthly love was suddenly *everywhere*! It was like Love and Happiness, and Peace and Comfort had bundled themselves together and descended upon me and my world until even the air I walked through seemed like pure *Love*.

Then I saw my younger brother, Jim, whom I adored, standing in our front yard waiting for us (having obviously escaped the watchful eye of our grandmother). And the Love that had descended upon me suddenly filled my heart with its' powerful love for him.

And I ran off to play with him, happy in my newfound knowledge that, truly, 'Someone Up There' loves us all very much!

And that makes us all very special indeed!

~ 32 ~

Love Won

*"For God sent not His Son into the world to
condemn the world, but that the world
through Him might be saved."*

(John 3:17)

THE day I went to Hollywood to shop for Hippie clothes, my heart still deeply loved that Love from Above I had felt as a child while walking home from school with my mother.

So when the Hippie Chick began quoting John 3:16 to me (*"For God so loved the world that He gave His Only Begotten Son, that Whosoever believes in Him should not perish but have eternal life"*), I took it as saying, in effect, that God is so **cruel** that He **forced** His Only Begotten Son to die for our sins!

And the moment she said it, I felt extremely protective of God. To me, God was *Love*. I had felt His Love come down on a sparkle

205

of light as a child. And even though I didn't know Who that God was, any suggestion that He was *other* than Love.....well, let's just say I felt sure that John 3:16 was defaming His Character!

I know better now, of course. But there were two things I didn't know back then that I know now:

First, *Jesus* is the Author of John 3:16 (and 17 as well, which says: *"For God sent not His Son into the world to condemn the world, but that the world through Him might be saved").*

Secondly, God the Father did not *force* Jesus to die for our sins! Jesus came of His *own free Will* to die on the Cross to save us! And to make sure we all understood this, He said:

> *"...I lay down My Life, that I may take it again.*
> *No man takes it from Me; but I lay it down OF MYSELF.*
>
> *I have Power to lay it down, and Power to take it again.*
> *This have I received of My [Heavenly] Father."*

(John 10:17-18)

See that? Jesus said, *"I lay down my Life, **no man** takes it from me. "* And, *wow*, do we ever see this played out in John 18:3-6!

As it happened, when Jesus was in the Garden of Gethsemane, praying to God the Father, a band of soldiers and officers arrived to get Him and bring Him before the chief priest and magistrates for judgment and crucifixion.

And knowing their purpose, Jesus got up from His prayer and went out to meet them, and He said to them: *"Whom do you seek?"*

"Jesus the Nazarene," they answered.

"I AM HE!" Jesus said. And, instantly, all the soldiers and officers fell *backward* to the ground!

Jesus is the Second Person of the Trinity of God – the Great 'I AM' – and His accusers couldn't even *stand* before Him. He had to *let them* get up and take Him away to be crucified!

Clearly, Jesus was not a Victim of anyone's will!

And neither was He a Victim of His Heavenly Father's Will! How do I know that? Look at what happened next:

Twelve Legions of Angels

When the soldiers and officers were getting up from the ground, Peter seized the moment, took out his sword, and cut off the high priest's servant's ear (John 18:10). Ouch!

And Merciful Jesus, ever our Compassionate Lord, immediately He reached out and restored the poor man's ear.

Then He turned to Peter and said, *"Put your sword back in its place…do you not think that I can now pray to My Father and He shall presently give Me more than twelve legions of angels [to save Me]?"* (Matthew 26:52-53).

Twelve legions of angels - let's see, according to the consensus on Google, that's anywhere from 3,000 to 6,000 per legion. So that's anywhere from thirty-six to seventy-two *thousand* angels!

And to put that amount of angelic power into perspective, just *one* angel could kick the whole world's backside if God so ordered it!

And here God would have sent *legions* of those dudes to save Jesus if He changed His Mind and didn't want to go through with the Cross.

But Jesus didn't change His Mind, did He!? He *wanted* to save us, and He came of *His own free Will* to do it!

For God So Loved the World

Of course, our Heavenly Father wanted to save us too! I'm sure His Heart was broken over our separation from Him.

And I'm also sure that's why, when Jesus spoke John 3:16 to the people, He immediately added: *"For God sent not His Son into the world to condemn the world, but that through Him the world might be saved"* (John 3:17).

Clearly, God the Father wanted to *save* us, not condemn us! We are so precious to Him that He *'gave'* us Jesus.

And the root form of that word **'gave'** there is particularly important! It means that in the same way an earthly father 'gives' his daughter's hand to her fiancé at the marriage altar, so God 'gave' Jesus His Blessing and Permission to come here and save us!

And this Blessing and Permission of God the Father was all-important to Jesus!

For as much as He wanted to save us (so much so that He would rather die than live without us), He would *not* have gone against His Heavenly Father's Will to do it!

How do I know that? Because He specifically said, *"I always do those things that please My Heavenly Father"* (John 8:29).

A Bloody Royal Battle

'But Kathy,' someone might ask me, *'what about those moments in the Garden of Gethsemane, when Jesus sweated great drops of Blood and prayed to God the Father to remove this cup from Him if there was any other way to save us?'*

I know. It sounds like Jesus didn't want to go through with the Cross, doesn't it!?

But here's the thing: Jesus was about to *become sin* on the Cross for our sakes! He was about to take the sin of the world *into Himself* and *become it* in order to kill it and bury it in His Grave.

And everything in His Holy Nature of Love was obviously recoiling at the reality of *becoming* such a wicked, hateful, horrid thing as *'sin.'*

209

*"He Who knew no sin **became sin** for us, that we might become the Righteousness of God in Him."*

(Second Corinthians 5:21)

Doing the Unimaginable

I've said it before, and I'll probably say it until I take my last breath - *sin is the **opposite** of God's Love.* The nature of sin is nothing but evil. And hate and cruelty beyond our imagination are intrinsic to its nature.

So here was Jesus, *the Love of God Personified,* getting ready to take ALL evil *into* Himself on the Cross and *become it*!

Can you imagine? Jesus was about to take all the vile, wicked, detestable, unimaginable sins that had ever been committed, past, present, and future, into His precious Holy Body of Love and BECOME IT!

He was about to suck every sin that had ever been committed on this planet – and every sin that ever would be - into His Holy Body, so that He could kill it all on the Cross and bury it in His Grave!

This had been the Plan of the Trinity of God from the Beginning, but now the time had come for Jesus to actually *do it.*

And the reality of it was so horrific to His Holy Nature of Love that, for a moment, His sinless Humanity shrank back, and He cried out, *'Father, if there's any other way, take this cup from Me.'*

~ 33 ~

Love and Connection

"God will redeem my soul from the power
of the grave and receive me."

(Psalm 49:15)

WHEN that Hippie Chick quoted John 3:16 to me, I had no idea that Jesus had come here of His own free Will to die for us. And I also didn't know about Second Corinthians 5:19, which informs us that *"God was in Christ, reconciling the world unto Himself."*

Meaning that all during Jesus' Life, and even on the Cross, God the Father was *with* Jesus, as well as *in* Jesus!

Only when Jesus 'became sin' on the Cross did His Heavenly Father leave Him. And then Jesus cried out what would have been our cry: *"My God, My God, why have you forsaken Me?"* (Matthew 27:46).

Of course, Jesus knew *'why.'* He knew all things, including all that He was going to experience here on Earth, all the way to the Cross and to Death (John 18:4).

But on the Cross, He was experiencing everything *we* would experience if He hadn't died for our sins and we hadn't had the opportunity to be born again with His Life. His cry would have been *our* cry: *'My God, my God, **WHY** have you forsaken me!?'*

Created for Connection

But here's a thought: Why would we ask God *"Why?"* Ah, the answer is in the way He created us!

Connection is a big deal with us, whether we realize it or not. Because 'connection' with the Trinity of God by way of God's Spirit living in our spirit is what we were *created for*, as the Bible reveals!

But alas, the Fall of Man broke that Divine Connection, demonstrated by God when He had an angel remove Adam and Eve from the Garden after they sinned.

As a result, we've ended up having to rely on one another for love and connection. But as important as our love for one another is (because it's God's design for our lives), human love is as a flickering candlelight compared to the full sunlight of God's Love!

Besides that, human love is not *Divine,* as no person is *God.* Moreover, it's not even possible for us to be connected to one another in the way that we were meant to be connected in Oneness to God.

Wired for Love

Oh, no doubt some people would scorn all this talk about 'love and connection.' But not only would they be denying how they were created; they would be denying the needs of their own heart as well.

Because as brain scientist Dr. Carolyn Leaf tells us in her awesome book, *Switch on Your Brain:* "Science is now able to demonstrate that we are wired for love."

"Science" says this? Yes! Aided by modern technology, scientists have discovered that our brain is *wired* for love, as Dr. Leaf carefully and technically explains in her book.

And this discovery comes not only from years of her own neurological and technological imaging research, but also from the findings of scientists all over the world (many of whom she references in her book).

Since the advent of computational computer programs, she explains, a plethora of human behavioral studies have been conducted worldwide to discover what is at the top of our 'needs' bucket list as people.

These studies were designed to discover things, like, what are people's most basic requirements for happiness? What gives people the psychological energy to get out of bed every day? What is the primary thing that we as people need to make us feel that life is worth living?

The largest of these studies involved thousands of participants (which would have been nearly impossible to conduct without the aid of modern technology).

And when all the questionnaires were completed and the participants' answers were technologically calculated through a special computer program, both the first *and* second place findings were unanimous!

In first place, one hundred percent of the participants' test scores revealed that their most important need in life is '*love.*'

And in second place, one hundred percent of the participants' scores revealed '*connection to others*' to be their second greatest need.

'*Love*' and '*Connection*' - top of our '*needs*' bucket list for happiness!

Through the Looking Glass

But the Bible has told us this already, hasn't it!? God knows how we tick, for He designed the clock.

And while we need to feel loved and connected with other people in a mutual love relationship, God designed us *first and foremost* to be loved by Him and connected to Him by His Spirit dwelling in our spirit.

In other words, God completes us.

Of course, I didn't know this before I met Jesus. But I *felt* it. And probably more so because of my red wagon experience.

Sitting there alone in the bushes that day, believing I was unloved and disconnected from everyone, that experience must have shown my soul what it was made for – *love* and *connection*.

And even though I apparently blocked out that traumatic experience from my memory at an early age, I can look back over my life and see how it informed my heart. For all my life, the main desire of my heart was always, *always* for love and connection, and I sought both *all the time*.

Above all, though, I *longed* for that Love I had felt as a child on the day I walked home from school with my mother. That Love was Happiness Itself, and it was so satisfying, so completely fulfilling, and made me feel so joyful in its Presence, that immediately I perceived it to be the Meaning of my life.

And because it had come down on a sparkle of light, I was ever thereafter attuned to the sunlight, always noticing how it lit up the flowers and foliage and sparkled on the ocean, how it moved across a room, warmed our world, illumined our days.

And though that Love had lasted only a short time and then was gone after I ran off to play with my brother, the sun showed up each morning as a comforting reminder of it and gave me hope for its return.

~ 34 ~

Shutting the Mouths of Lions

"Then Daniel said unto king [Darius]...
'My God has sent His angel, and has shut the
lions' mouths, that they have not hurt me...'

So Daniel was taken up out of the den
and no manner of hurt was found upon him,
because he believed in his God."

(Daniel 6:21-23)

IN a secret place in our heart and mind, it seems we all hold an image of an idyllic existence. Far from the lions' den that Daniel was thrown into, it is a place of love and beauty, great happiness, and nothing to fear.

And as it happened, I got to experience that idyllic place for a few amazing moments as a child, when I felt God's Love coming down on a sparkle of light.

221

"In Your Presence, O God, is fullness of joy;
at Your Right Hand are pleasures forevermore."

(Psalm 16:11)

And not surprisingly, that wonderful Presence of God's Love I felt became what I would ever thereafter think of as my 'happy place.' And the memory of it stayed with me always.

And I would need that memory! For once Satan had succeeded in assaulting my self-worth through my red wagon experience, then evil spirits continued using that same tactic on me over and over, non-stop throughout the ensuing years.

Satanic Tactics

I don't know if you've ever been bullied (and who hasn't, to one degree or another?). But along with suffering the various kinds of pain and sorrow and fear that come with life in this fallen world, I was never without some girl assaulting my self-worth.

Whether it was the ongoing negative insults of my childhood playmate who'd ditched me in the bushes (as we were together often during our childhood)......

......or it was some girl at school rolling her eyes at me, or making snide remarks about me to the other kids, or laughing at me in front of others for no apparent reason, it was like I was the standout duck in the pond to take shots at.

222

I understand it now, of course. We are made in God's Image and Likeness; therefore, Satan is so jealous of us, he can't stand any of us having any self-worth at all.

So Satan commands his evil spirits to continually work at exercising their power over the evil part of our fallen good and evil natures, trying to cause us to say and do things that hurt one another; things which often, later on, we're sorry for saying and doing.

And this is exactly what the Apostle Paul was talking about when he wrote: *"For we wrestle not against flesh and blood, but against principalities, against [evil] powers, against the rulers of the darkness of this world and spiritual wickedness in high places"* (Ephesians 6:12).

God had revealed to Paul the reality of demonic activity in this world. And once educated by God about it, Paul proceeded to write about it and teach us how to respond to it: *"Put on the whole armor of God, that you may be able to stand against the wiles of the devil"* (Ephesians 6:11).

But I didn't know anything about that when I was being insulted and bullied during my adolescent and teenage years, because I didn't yet have Jesus' Life dwelling within me.

So I couldn't think with the Mind of Christ – "the Helmet of Salvation" - regarding my True Identity.

And I couldn't use the Truth of the Word of God – "the Sword of the Spirit" - to cut through all the bullies' lies about my self-worth and stand on the wonderful facts that God says about me in His Word.

Neither could I put on the "Breastplate of Righteousness" – the Holiness of Jesus given to us as a free Gift from God when we receive His Life.

No, I didn't yet have the Armor of God to 'wear.'

But I had the memory of God's Love from Above to sustain me.

That Love I felt while walking home from school with my mother had made me feel so valuable, that the very memory of it was like a shield about my heart and mind that kept me from tearing at myself.

And just as *"the King always has one more move,"* there came a time when the bullying was at such a fever pitch, that God let me feel His Love once again.

And whereas the first time His Love had come down on a sparkle of light, this time it came through music.....

.

224

~ 35 ~

Trying to Fly Home

"And I said, O that I had wings like a dove!
for then would I fly away and be at rest."

(Psalm 55:6)

THE consensus of the Psalmists is that *'in all the world there is none like You, O God, and no love like Yours.'* And I experienced this once again about God's Love when I was around ten.

It happened near the city of Los Angeles, in Southern California. Back then, in the late 1950's, the L.A. basin and its outlying areas were really quite rural and lovely. Much of the area's natural vegetation had yet to be replaced by the vast urban growth we see today, and the sky was so blue, it felt like you could reach up and touch it on a whim.

Also, flowering bushes were everywhere - roses, camelias, hydrangeas, and, of course, those jolly hibiscus with their big orange and red, and pink and yellow flowers that bloomed nine months out

225

of the year. These were a delight to visitors from colder states where winter storms often froze the vegetation or blocked out the flora's necessary light with a blanket of snow for months on end.

Not so in balmy Southern California! There, one could find mild winters, streets lined with palm trees, and sprawling green lawns joined end-to-end in front of Spanish, Mediterranean, and Early California-style homes.

Blue Skies

I was at one of those homes when God let me feel His Love again. It was my Aunt Helen's home, and visiting her was one of my favorite things to do during summer vacation.

I loved kicking back on her front lawn and watching the tall palm trees sway their hellos to the passing clouds.

And I loved that she lived just a few miles from the Pacific Ocean, and only one short block from a large park replete with a concert bowl and public swimming pool.

What great fun it was when my mom and Aunt Helen would pack a picnic basket, load all of us kids - my brother, two sisters, two cousins and me - with towels and balls and swimsuits, and then lead us all down the street to that wonderful park. It was kiddie heaven!

Oh, the joy of eating watermelon and chocolate cake, of swimming in the pool with a hundred other crazy kids and getting purple Popsicles from the ice cream stand!

Sometimes when my dad and uncle joined us on the weekend, we'd stay long into the evening, roasting hot dogs and hamburgers to the lilting sound of music floating over from the concert bowl.

Then we would all walk home under the stars, satiated with the pleasures of the day.

The Sound of Love

It was on one of those summer days that I once again experienced God's Love. It began when my Aunt Helen sat down at her piano and played the most beautiful piece of classical music I'd ever heard.

At first it sounded like just another lovely song. But soon the music became more distinctive......and *romantic*.

The bass notes began sending little overtures to the treble notes, and they in turn responded shyly, trilling out soft cadences and sweet arpeggios in the manner of a blushing beauty.

Slowly, reservedly at first, the bass and treble made their acquaintance. But soon reticence gave way to inspiration, and their communication grew more beautiful and intense.

The bass became more masculine, passionate, and gorgeous. And the treble, charmed and emboldened by it, began revealing the exquisite beauties of its delicate harmonies.

Intently I listened as they played their music, more and more unabashedly communicating with one another, sweetly, harmoniously, magnificently; each inspiring the other to greater heights of expression. It was as if they were talking, laughing, praying…...and falling in love.

The Voice of God

Such enchanted moments these were! Me sitting on the floor, my mother resting on the sofa nearby, both of us enraptured, our hearts soaring with the music that filled the room.

And what happened next, I can't explain, but as I listened, suddenly there came the most beautiful Voice, like one would imagine could only be the Voice of God, singing a passionate Song of Love to me and to the world through the music.

Oh, I didn't hear it with my natural ears, but I didn't need to. When God speaks to us by His Spirit, His Voice is infinitely more Real and Alive than any earthly voice.

And when I heard it, whether in my mind or by His Spirit, it was filled with so much Love for all of us that, instantly, I was filled with joy!

And everything in me responded to it so passionately in return, that my heart felt like a glowing sun burning within me, trying with its rays to reach out to that Love, to rise to it, to embrace it.

But I wasn't able. As strong as my desire was, it could not reach beyond the walls of my humanity. So I just sat there, tears of joy and longing streaming down my cheeks, amazed that aside from the shedding of a few tears and the utterance of a few words of praise for my aunt's ability to play such beautiful music, no other avenue of expression was available to me. Unless I wanted to get up and dance.

Longing

I think that was the first time I consciously realized that my capacity to rise to God was beyond my own ability. Such tremendous potential seemed to be within me, and yet strangely, it all seemed to be held captive within my body.

I didn't know back then that my spirit was the place where God and my soul were meant to be united.

All I knew was that the Love from Above I had felt years earlier as I was walking home from kindergarten with my mother - *that* Love had just sung a passionate Song of Love to me and to the world through my Aunt Helen's music.

And I had responded....like a homing pigeon, one leg tied to the ground, trying to fly Home.

229

~ 36 ~

I Will Lead the Blind by a Way
They Knew Not

"I will lead the blind by a way they knew not:
I will lead them in paths they have not known;
I will make darkness light before them,
and crooked things straight."

(Isaiah 42:16)

BY the time I was twenty-four, I was married with children. I had a handsome husband, one darling son, and two precious stepchildren, all of whom I loved.

But nothing I had experienced of life in this fallen world had been sufficient to fill that empty hole I'd always felt deep within me.

I wasn't knowledgeable about what had happened to us in the Fall of Man, so I didn't know that that empty hole was the absence of God dwelling in my spirit, where my soul was meant to be connected to Him, but I was feeling the effects of His absence. There was something terribly missing in my life; and try as I did to fill it with people, places and things, the emptiness remained.

Oswald Chambers wrote, *"It is by the heart that God is perceived."*

And the only times my heart had felt completely happy and whole were those two occasions when I felt God's Love as a child, which I've shared with you.

But things took a dramatic turn the year I turned twenty-four. By then my inner emptiness had become unbearable. And as it happened, one Sunday morning I woke up with a strong desire to go to church. And not to just any church. I wanted to go to the little one located about half a block from where I lived.

I'd always admired how the building had floor-to-ceiling windows on both sides, and how it was tucked under a stand of tall Eucalyptus trees, and how there were flowers and ferns decorating the perimeter, hugging the building.

Occasionally, I'd entertained the idea of attending a Sunday service there, the outer setting being so pretty and all, and I was curious to see what the inside was like. But I'd never wanted to go to a Christian church bad enough to actually *go*.

Well, now I wanted to go - and not just to see the décor. I wanted to hear what the pastor had to say about God. And so I called to find

~ 37 ~

Ten Minutes is All I Ask

"When the poor and needy seek water, and there is none,
and their tongue [their soul] fails for thirst, I, the Lord,
will hear them; I, the God of Israel, will not forsake them.

I will open rivers in high places, and fountains in the
midst of valleys; I will make the wilderness a pool of water,
and dry land springs of water."

(Isaiah 41:17-18)

Not long after my visit to the little garden church, I met up with some friends at a restaurant one afternoon. Their companionship was good, and the conversation was lively. But that day something hard to describe occurred within me.

About a half hour into our visit, suddenly my perception changed, and I 'saw' that our conversation barely touched the surface of our existence.

237

And suddenly a desperation for God rose to a fever pitch within me. It was like I had been racing through the shallow waters of life, doing this, that and the other, trying in vain to find fulfillment, and suddenly I hit a wall and didn't want to go on without God. I wanted to know Him and to communicate with Him, and to have Him in my life forever.

I didn't say anything to my friends about what I was feeling; I only wanted to talk to God about it. I wanted to ask Him how I could know Him and be united somehow in a relationship with Him.

Not that I knew if such a uniting was possible, but I felt like there had to be a way. The pastor of the little garden church had explained how we could open our hearts to Jesus and invite Him in, and I'd done that. But so far I was just the same ol' empty me.

The God Who Sees

Psalm 94:9 says, *"He that planted the ear, shall He not hear? He that formed the eye, shall He not see?"*

And as I sat there, half-listening to my friends' conversation, suddenly it was as if someone switched on a light in my brain, and I realized that the God Who had created my mind *also had a Mind!* And in that moment, I *knew* He was hearing what I was thinking!

And with that, suddenly I sensed the Presence of the Mind of God there with me. I don't know how to convey this, but suddenly the Mind of God was there and more real than all the people in the restaurant, including my friends.

So I wasted no time. Quickly, silently, I said something like, '*I know You can hear me.....please come to me, please give me just ten minutes of your time.....I need to talk to you.....I need to know Who You are, and why I'm living here in this world without You. Please come to me, ten minutes is all I ask.*'

I've never forgotten those words; they are etched onto my mind and heart even now. For they came from the depths of my being and were the most honest, desperate words I'd ever spoken.

But then, unbelievably, I put conditions on my request! I said to God, '*Please don't send any people to me in Your place. I've heard from people. Now I just want to talk to You.*'

And at that, I perceived that God nodded '*Yes.*' And I knew that the God of the universe had just granted my request.

I was going to have my ten minutes.

~ *38* ~

A Little Child Shall Lead Them

"And Jesus said, Let the little children come unto Me:
for of such is the Kingdom of Heaven."

(Matthew 19:14)

EACH day after my request in the coffee shop, I waited for God to reach down from Heaven and say, *"Okay, Kathy, you've got ten minutes."*

And about three days or so into my waiting, one afternoon I was driving home with my youngest son sitting next to me on the passenger seat. And out of the blue, he said, *'Mama, if I tell you something, will you promise not to laugh at me?'*

'Of course, I promise,' I assured him. *'I would never laugh at you!'* After a moment of silence, I glanced over at my son, and by the look on his little face, I realized that he was trying to drum up his courage to confide in me.

I waited quietly. Then with great hesitation, he slowly said: '*Last night....after I went to bed....a man came into my room and talked with me.*'

Whoa! Stifling my consternation, I said, '*How did he get in, honey?*'

I couldn't imagine how. We lived in an apartment on the third floor of the building (the first floor a parking garage).

And the only way in or out of our apartment was either through the front door or the patio door, both of which opened to the living room. And my husband and I had been sitting in the living room until late that night.

I looked over at my little boy. Now he was squinting his forehead, obviously trying to find the words to explain to me how this 'man' got into his room.

'*Well,*' he said slowly, '*first my room lit up like it was daytime, and then the wall where the window is disappeared into the bright light . . . and that's where he came in.*'

My mind raced. I'd always hated anything to do with the occult, and especially the idea of dead people coming to visit. But I had to be gracious to my son by not showing my alarm.

(At this point, dear reader, you may have noticed that I haven't put this conversation with my son in direct quotation marks. That's because I'm recalling it from memory, not from one of my diaries. And although I still remember the conversation like it was yesterday,

I can't say that I'm writing it exactly as it was spoken, although I believe I am - such a conversation is hard to forget!)

Anyway, drumming up my most stoic attitude, I said to my little boy, '*And you said that this man talked to you?*'

I glanced over and saw that he was looking at me, sort of sideways out of the corner of his eye, as if trying to discern whether or not I believed him. So I smiled at him, as if to say: 'See, honey, I believe you. I'm not laughing.'

The smile seemed to put him at ease, and he said, '*Yes, he talked to me. When he came in, he was smiling at me, like he was happy to see me. And after saying hello, he sat down at the end of my bed, and we talked.*'

Oh, how I hated this. '*What did you talk about?*' I asked.

'*Mmm,*' he said, trying to recall the order of conversation. '*Well, first we talked about my school.....he asked me how I liked it and what I liked best about it. And then we talked about fishing.*' (My son loves to fish.)

'*Were you afraid?*' I asked him.

'*Oh no,*' he said, '*it was real peaceful, I felt happy.*'

At that point, I must have had a look on my face that said I believed him, because he quickly, enthusiastically added, '*He even tucked High Pockets in bed with me, mama!*'

'High Pockets' was an adorable stuffed animal that a friend of my mother's had made and given him for Christmas a few months before. And I remember being moved in my heart that this 'man' had been mothering my child by talking with him and tucking his favorite stuffed animal in bed with him, whereas I hadn't done either.

'Then what happened, son?' I asked him.

To this day I vividly remember how my little boy gazed off for a moment, scrunching his forehead again, as if he were trying to remember exactly what had happened next.

'Well,' he said slowly, *'I guess I fell asleep while we were talking, because I don't remember him leaving. When I woke up this morning, he was gone.'*

A Little Child Shall Lead them

Seeing the seriousness on my son's face and how difficult it was for him to tell me these things moved my heart.

And the last thing I wanted to do was make him think that I didn't believe him, or that I was dismissing his experience by not asking him the next appropriate question.

So even though I didn't want to hear the answer, I said: *'Did you know who the man was, honey?'*

At this, he scooted to the edge of his seat and turned to face me. Putting his right arm on the dashboard to steady himself in the moving car (we didn't have seatbelts back then), he said: *'Yes, I knew him.'*

244

'Who was he, son?' I asked.

Looking directly into my eyes now, as if he were no longer a child but some ancient of days who could see deep into my soul, he said:

'It was JESUS!'

And at the Name of *JESUS*, a power came from his words that gently pushed my head back into the headrest, and with that, something like a veil made of scales fell off my inner eyes, and I knew the Truth: that Jesus is the Son of God Who died for our sins, and that He had appeared to my son in answer to my prayer to know God!

Not Prepared for House Guests

My next thought was one of panic: *'Oh, my gosh, I wonder if his room is clean!'*

I had been expecting the Mind of God to tap on my consciousness and say, "Okay, Kathy, here I am, you've got ten minutes." *Not God to come walking into my house!*

By this time, I was pulling into our parking garage, and as I turned off the car, I assured my son that I believed him.

Then I gathered our things and rushed up the stairs to our apartment, practically dragging the little guy by his hand as I went.

Entering our home, I rushed to my son's bedroom and threw open the door. *Whew* - it was neat and tidy! (Oh, the mercies of God!) And there was High Pockets, still tucked under the covers.

245

Immediately then I rushed into my own bedroom and threw myself on my knees beside the bed. Clasping my hands together on the bedspread, I buried my face in them and prayed:

'Jesus! I'm so sorry! I'm sorry that I rejected that Hippie who tried to tell me about You.....I'm sorry I didn't believe in You back then. I don't understand why You had to die for my sins. I don't understand what Your Cross was all about. But whatever You did there, I accept it. Please come to me! I need You.....I know now that You are the Son of God come down from Heaven as God. Please come to me!'

I've never forgotten those words; they are etched into my heart and mind. And because Jesus had visited my little son *in Person*, I thought that was the way it had to happen with me.

So I prayed again, wanting to make sure that He heard me and understood that I was serious:

'Jesus, I give You my life. I understand now that you are God. Please come to me.....I want to know You, I want You to be in my life! I need You!'

I don't know how long I waited there, kneeling beside my bed, hoping Jesus was hearing me. But soon a wonderful peace swept over me, and I knew that He was coming. I didn't know how or when, but I knew that He had heard my prayer and that He was coming.

~ 39 ~

The Appointed Time and Place

"Ah, Lord God! You have made Heaven and Earth
by Your great Power...and there is
nothing too hard for You."

(Jeremiah 32:17)

A FEW days passed by while I waited for Jesus, keeping my great expectations to myself, telling no one of our upcoming meeting. I didn't know when or where He would appear, and I didn't think about what I might be wearing.

When Jesus looked on me, I wanted Him to see me as I really was - a girl who desperately needed to be united to the True and Living God. And I was already dressed within for that occasion.

Well, as it happened, about a week into my waiting, my mom called and asked if I would chaperone my seventeen-year-old sister, Pam, and her girlfriend as they drove from Orange County (where we

247

lived in Southern California) to Redwood City, near San Francisco in Northern California. We would be seeing our dad, brother, and married sister and her children for Easter vacation.

Of course, I knew the trip would delay my meeting with Jesus for at least a week. But I also knew that I shouldn't be selfish. So I agreed, and a few days later we packed up the car and made the eight hour trip to Redwood City.

The week went by quickly, and we had a nice time with our family. Then, on our last day, Easter Sunday, we went to church with some cousins. There, I took communion for the first time, and as I chewed the bread and drank the grape juice, I prayed silently, confirming to Jesus that I was serious about wanting Him in my life.

Planning the Trip Home

That afternoon, Pam pulled me aside to discuss our trip home. She said she wanted to make it a leisurely trip and stop for an overnight stay at the Big Sur campgrounds along the ocean. Which sounded like great fun to me, so we made it a plan.

Then she said, '*Kathy, on our way to Big Sur, I want to show you one of the most beautiful places I've ever seen. This place will blow your mind!*'

'*Where is it?*' I asked.

'*It's in the redwood-covered foothills just above the ocean, about thirty minutes from here.*'

248

Pam is a nature lover of the first order, so I knew I was in for a sight. Of course, I had no expectations that Jesus would meet with me there, because the girls would be with me.

Still though, I was excited to see this 'beautiful place' she had described.

A New Day

Early the next morning we were all packed up and on the road, and it looked to be a perfect day. The early morning light was soft and golden, and the spring air was clean and scented with freshness.

Pam drove expertly out of the city and onto a two-lane road that climbed gently until it reached some woodlands not far from the ocean.

After a little while, she slowed the car to a crawl and began looking for the trail that led to her 'beautiful place.'

I rolled down my backseat window and breathed in the scented air. The spring grass and wildflowers growing alongside the road glistened with dew in the early morning light, and already I could see that the area was lovely.

Suddenly, Pam pulled over and stopped the car on the side of the road. *'There it is!'* she exclaimed, looking intently into the trees and a tall stand of foliage.

'Where?' I said, *'I don't see anything.'*

'*It's over there, hidden by the overgrowth,*' she said, pointing to an opening in the trees. '*It's a trail - an old fire road actually - leading to the top of the hill, but the view of the ocean from up there is worth the hike.*'

Excitedly, we bounded out of the car and tromped around in the foliage until we found the trail. And then we began to climb......

~ 40 ~

Born Again

"My voice shalt Thou hear in the morning, O Lord;
in the morning will I direct my prayer unto Thee,
and will look up."

(Psalm 5:3)

LESS than a quarter mile into our hike, I saw a bit of color flash through the thick stand of tall ferns and redwood trees on the right of the trail. Curious, I pushed aside a couple of the fern fronds and saw a beautiful little valley not far below.

'Hey girls,' I said, *'look at this!'*

'I know,' said Pam, *'it's beautiful, isn't it? I've been down there, a little stream runs through it!'*

'Well, you girls go on ahead, I have to see this place!' I pushed back the ferns and began walking-slipping-sliding down the slope, uprooting miniature plants and scuffing little rocks from their hollows

251

along the way. Behind me, Pam said, *'I'll call you when we come back down the mountain...don't go too far away!'*

But her words barely registered in my mind for the joy of my happy thoughts: *'Jesus will meet me here! This is where He will come to me!'*

The Beautiful Valley

Soon I was on the valley floor, running out into the middle of it, looking for the little water brook Pam spoke of. *'Ah, yes, here it is,'* I thought happily, *'it's like a little babbling brook.'*

Turning around slowly to see the full view of the valley, charmed by its 360 degrees of beauty, it was like something I had imagined seeing in Heaven.

Decorative trees graced the valley floor here and there, and a carpet of bright green grass laced with patches of wildflowers sparkled with morning dew.

Oh, what great expectations I had as I sat down beside the little brook and waited for Jesus! Oh, the joy that filled my heart as I took in the beauty around me!

Bliss was mine; I owned it now. Butterflies came by to see if I was a flower, and the birds sang joyfully as they flitted from tree to tree. Beside me, the little brook sounded like music as the water trickled over the small rocks.

'Here I am, Jesus,' I said. *'This place is beautiful, maybe a little like Heaven, so it's a good place for You to come to me.'*

Sweet Reverie

Waiting for Jesus, I quietly sang a little hymn about Him that I'd heard my mother sing many times (entitled *In the Garden),* about coming to a garden alone when the dew is fresh in the morning, and hearing the Voice of Jesus, which is so sweet even the birds stop their singing and listen.

Then I sang the song's refrain – *"And He walks with me, and He talks with me, and He tells me I am His own..."*

After that, I recited what little I knew of the 23rd Psalm:

> *"The Lord is my Shepherd, I shall not lack.*
> *He makes me to lie down in green pastures,*
> *He leads me beside the still waters.*
> *He restores my soul."*

Looking happily around, then lounging back on the grass and gazing into the blue sky, and then sitting up and looking happily around again, I watched and listened for Jesus.

Oh, how sweetly time passed as I waited for Him! I knew I was in the perfect place to meet with the One Who had created all nature.

A Voice Calling

Time passed blissfully. Then more time passed. And *finally,* a voice! Calling my name! I jumped up and looked around for Jesus.

But it wasn't Him......it was Pam. Waving her hand to me from the top of the trail. *"Kathy,"* she called out. *"It's time to go now."*

Stunned

'No...this can't be!' I thought, desperately looking around the valley for Jesus. Obviously, time had stood still in my mind while I'd waited for Him to arrive. I hadn't noticed that the dew had evaporated, and the golden morning sunlight had turned white and beat down harder.

And now it was time to go. I stared at Pam, trying to comprehend what was happening. Again, she waved and called out, *"It's time to go now!"*

Numb

Slowly, laboriously, I began the trek across the valley floor toward the girls. My legs felt like stone, and my mind was in shock.

About halfway across the valley, a sudden realization dawned on me: *'If Jesus wouldn't meet with me here in this most beautiful place, He's not going to meet with me anywhere.'*

When I finally reached the slope and began the hard climb back up to the trail, another thought dawned on me: *'Jesus had probably never planned on coming to me because I rejected that Hippie Chick when she tried to tell me about Him!'*

'Why should He come now, just because I'm ready?' I reasoned. *'When He was ready, I wouldn't have anything to do with Him. Now it's too late.'*

Oh, the ineffable sadness that washed over me as I struggled to get back up the slope. '*I never really had a word or promise from Him that He would come to me,*' I thought. '*It was my own mind, my own wishful thinking that made me believe He would.*'

Chasing Sheep

When I finally reached the top of the slope and was pushing back the ferns, I heard Pam yell out, *"SHEEP!!"* And I stepped onto the trail just in time to see her and her friend chasing some sheep down the road, running lickity-split toward our car.

What a comical sight! Pam's long blond hair flying, her friend's curly brown hair bouncing, the sheep running for their lives, all of them enveloped in a great cloud of dust. Instinctively, I moved to run after them, but before I even got going, a Voice boomed out of the sky above me, saying,

"MY SHEEP SHALL KNOW MY VOICE!"

And I looked up just in time to see a bright light shoot down through the redwood trees on the other side of the road from the beautiful valley, and then *THERE HE WAS!! JESUS! Standing in front of me in a blazing Light of Glory and Majesty and Beauty indescribable! And He was holding His Hands out to me and smiling, as if He was joyful to see me!*

And in that moment, I was shot through with joy, and I cried out, *"Master!"* just as my knees were buckling. I would have fallen if His Power hadn't held me up.

255

I called Him *"Master"* because I *knew Him.* Like a baby kidnapped and suffering from amnesia might get its memory back the moment it was returned to its mother's arms, so I *knew* Jesus!

He is our Beloved Lord and Master, the King of Heaven and Earth and all there is, and somehow, somewhere in time and eternity past, I had known Him. I had *always* known Him.

And seeing Him now, standing in front of me in an indescribable Blaze of Love and Glory, my whole being was instantly filled with a joy that was pure ecstasy!

Our Glorious King

I wish I could perfectly describe Him here, but there is nothing on Earth to compare Him to. Unmistakably, all the power and beauty of nature, and the sun, moon, and stars above had their originating point in His Glorious Face, which was *Love.*

And emanating from the Light of His entire Being was the most Glorious, Fulfilling *Love,* beyond anything I'd ever imagined or felt. And His Beautiful Smile told me that He was as happy to see me as I was to see Him!

As to His hair, it seemed to be brown and shoulder length. But I didn't look at it directly; I didn't look away from His Loving Face (which appeared to be made from some Heavenly bronze ore, as if it had been hewn from some celestial rock mountain, and yet His skin was pliable like a human's face).

256

As to His Clothing, it seemed as if He wore a white gown, but He was surrounded in such a blaze of Light, which 'seemed' to emanate from within Him, it was like His Clothing was made of Light.

And although His Light was brighter than the sun, with bits of transparent colors radiating within it and around Him, as if dancing for joy, it didn't hurt my eyes; paradoxically there was a softness to it that allowed me to look directly at Him.

And His Beautiful Face and His Light were pure *Love.* I could feel His Love-Light on my skin and within my whole being. And the moment I saw Him, I was shot through with a joy that was pure ecstasy!

And immediately I threw my arms out to Him and tried to step toward Him, to embrace Him; and He moved toward me, His Arms already being stretched out to me, *and then He and His Love-Light went right into me!*

And just like that, I was filled with His Life! A Life so joyful, so freeing, so Complete Love, that the feeling of it was out of this world! Gone now was the emptiness in my heart. Gone were the cold walls in my soul that had once felt so hard and dead because I was separated within from God.

In place of those cold, hard walls, I can't explain it, but it felt like a soft Heavenly Flower had been placed in my inner being - no stems, no thorns, just softness and beauty, and like fresh oxygen from Heaven had been breathed into me.

And after a few moments of sweet communion with Him, His Power turned me and sent me running down the trail to catch up with the girls. (I was their chaperone, and He was sending me to look after them.)

And as I ran, filled with joy about Jesus, I was in a state of wonderment about His Life now dwelling within me, because I'd never known such a thing could happen to a person.

And as I ran, wondering, a Beautiful Presence filled the sky above me, which I immediately knew to be the Presence of God, because the feeling was the same as that Love I had experienced coming down on a sparkle of light as a child, and a Voice said, *"You've been born again!"*

And I thought, *"AGAIN? I never knew a person could be born AGAIN! Nobody ever told me about this!"*

And then I arrived at the bottom of the trail and found the girls standing by the car, laughing. They'd had great fun chasing the sheep (which were now nowhere in sight), and I was so happy, I laughed with them.

"Sing, O Daughter, and shout;
be glad and rejoice with all your heart,
for the Lord your God in the midst of you is Mighty."

(Zephaniah 3:14, 17)

TRUTH

Part III

Clothed Upon with Truth

~ 41 ~

A New Creation in Christ Jesus

"If any [girl] is in Christ, [she] is a New Creation;
old things are passed away, and behold,
all things are become new."

(Second Corinthians 5:17)

YOU'VE heard of gifts in disguise, right? Well, it's not lost on me that the distressing things I endured growing up were actually gifts in disguise, because they drove me to Jesus!

Desperate for relief from the emptiness within me, which I felt in the world as well, I gladly embraced Jesus and received His Life!

I liken it to what happens in the cocoon of a caterpillar. In order for the little belly-crawling lowlander to be transformed into its full potential and become a beautiful butterfly, there's a life-or-death struggle within it that must take place.

I once heard a scientist talking about this on the radio. As a boy, he spotted a butterfly struggling to get out of its cocoon, and feeling sorry for the little creature, he pulled out his pocketknife and carefully slit the cocoon open to set it free.

But instead of flying away, the butterfly just laid there, weakly flapping its wings until, sadly, it died.

Well, of course, the boy felt terrible. Though he was just a child, he knew that somehow he had caused the butterfly's demise. Which, in fact, he did, as he would eventually learn in high school science.

A butterfly's struggle in its cocoon is critical. The constant pressure of its body pushing against the walls of the cocoon causes a protein called 'chitin' to be excreted into the soft skeletal structure of the butterfly's newly formed wings.

And when this chitin solidifies, it hardens this skeletal structure of the wings (like the wooden frames of paper kites we fly on windy days), and that's how the butterfly gets 'lift off.'

The Secret Value of Struggle

All that is how I view my life-struggles, which ultimately caused me to seek Jesus. Rather than destroying me, they had what I call 'the butterfly effect' on me.

Meaning, that all along the Lord had been working in the midst of my emptiness and tribulations to develop me into a person who desired to know and be united to the True and Living God above all else.

And this desire caused me to seek God, open my heart to Jesus and be set free from the death-to-God consequences of the Fall of Man by receiving His Life.

The Garments of Salvation

And, oh, what a Glorious Life! A Beautiful Divine Life that empowers all who receive it to live and soar in the Presence of Heaven's Royalty, not with the puny power of butterfly wings (metaphorically speaking), but with the power of eagle's wings, as God's Word uses the metaphor in Isaiah 40:31, saying:

"They that wait on the Lord shall renew their strength,
they shall mount up with wings as eagles,
they shall run and not be weary; and
they shall walk and not faint."

And soaring on wings was how I felt as I ran down the mountain trail after meeting Jesus! My feet were on the ground running, but my heart and mind and soul were soaring with the joy of His Glorious Life now dwelling within me!

Isaiah 61:10 says:

"I will greatly rejoice in the Lord; my soul is joyful in my God: for He has clothed me with the Garments of Salvation, He has covered me with the Robe of Righteousness, as a bridegroom decks himself with ornaments, and as a bride adorns herself with her jewels."

And 'greatly rejoicing' was the state of my whole being when I met up with the girls at the bottom of the mountain trail after meeting Jesus! And after laughing with them about the sheep, we all jumped into the car and hit the road again. Soon we were traveling alongside the ocean.

I was in the backseat, filled with thoughts of Jesus and His Presence now within me, and astounded at how He had 'downloaded' (to use computer language) such an immense amount of information about Himself, that it was as if I had been walking and talking with Him forever. And He is *INCREDIBLE!!!*

And as I pondered on this as we drove along, what happened next is hard for me to adequately explain. But as I gazed out the window at the sea, *'Reality'* opened to me, and I saw our world enveloped by the glowing Presence of God, Who is *Love.* The sky, the land, the sea – *everything* was surrounded by the Presence of God.

In the same way a pregnant woman's body surrounds the baby in her womb, so I saw that the Earth is encompassed by the Living God, Who is, in fact, Three Beings – God the Father, God the Son, and God the Holy Spirit. And even though They are Three Beings, They are One in Heart and Mind and in every other respect, as I saw.

Just as the sun we see in the sky is comprised of a physical ball of fire (think God the Father); and that fire creates light (think Jesus, "the Light of the world" and "the Brightness of God's Glory"); and the sunlight shines down to us through the conduit of 'rays' (think the Holy Spirit), so I saw the Divine Presence and Relationship of the Trinity of God - Heaven's Royalty.

And They are *Love!* And They are *everywhere,* just as I would one day read in Psalm 138:8-10, which says:

> *"Where shall I go from Your Spirit?*
> *Or where shall I flee from Your Presence?*
>
> *If I ascend up into Heaven, You are there,*
> *if I make my bed in hell, behold, You are there.*
>
> *If I take the wings of the morning,*
> *and dwell in the uttermost parts of the sea,*
>
> *even there shall Your Hand lead me,*
> *and Your right Hand shall hold me."*

And as I stared in awe at the Reality of our Living Triune God, hot tears of joy and *relief* (because God is LOVE*)* rose from deep within me and streamed silently down my cheeks.

And straightway there came the most incredible sweet communication from God to my heart that made my tears of joy flow even hotter on my cheeks.

I'd spent my whole life envisioning God as in Heaven where the dead people are. But now I saw that our Three-Person God is the *Living* God, and the God of the *living.*

And They are not just in Heaven, They are *everywhere,* and They are *with* us (as I would later learn that Jesus' Name "Immanuel" means "God *with* us").

God is Love, God is Light, God is Joy, God is Beauty, God has all Power. And as the Holy Son of God, Jesus is *the Brightness of God's Glory and the Exact Image of His Person, the One Who upholds all things by the Word of His Power"* (Hebrews 1:3). And I saw this for myself.

Thy Word is Truth

At some point during this wonderful vision of Reality, I became aware that God wanted me to look at the small Bible I had brought along for the trip. So I pulled it out of my bag and opened it randomly, not knowing where to begin.

And as God would have it, the pages opened to John 3:3, where Nicodemus, a Pharisee, had sneaked around behind the other Pharisees backs at night to question Jesus on eternal life and other spiritual matters.

And immediately Jesus told him that in order to enter the Kingdom of God, we must be *"born again."* And when I saw those words, I just stared at them. Totally floored that my own experience of being born again was not only recorded in the Bible but spoken of by *Jesus Himself!*

Nicodemus, of course, was befuddled as to how a person could possibly be born AGAIN. And he said to Jesus: *"How can a man be born when he is old? Can he enter his mother's womb and be born a second time?"*

And Jesus answered him *prophetically.* In advance of His Cross and Resurrection (after which He would be giving us His Divine Life on the Day of Pentecost), He said to Nicodemus:

"Except a man is born of water
[Jesus is the Water of Life – John 4:7-14]
and of the Spirit [of God],
he cannot enter the Kingdom of God.

That which is born of the flesh is flesh,
and that which is born of the Spirit is spirit. "

And when I read that, I was like, 'Oh-h-h, so *that's* how it works! There's a physical birth and a spiritual birth: I was physically born of my human mother and father, and now I have been spiritually born of God through Jesus! '

And I was blown away that, here I was, my very own witness to the Truth of what Jesus had said to Nicodemus!

~ *42* ~

The Door to God

"And Jesus said, 'I am the Door [to God]:
by Me, if any [girl] enters in, [she] shall be saved.' "

(John 10:9)

HAVE you seen *The Truman Show?* It's a movie about a guy named Truman who was cast as the main character in a reality sitcom when he was just a baby. But he didn't know it. Nobody told him.

Consequently, he grew up thinking that he was experiencing real life, when actually he was just living on a movie set and all the people around him were actors.

And to make matters worse, there were hidden cameras everywhere, broadcasting his every move - *live*, on television, where the rest of the world could tune in and watch his life evolving like a soap opera.

269

Well, as fortune would have it, one day Truman discovered the hoax. I don't remember exactly how, but something caught his attention and he figured it out. And the movie ends with him finding the exit door leading to the outside world and walking through it to begin his *real* life.

And that's how I see my life before I met Jesus: Just as Truman grew up living a duped life on a phony sitcom, but he didn't know it, and then one day he escaped through the exit door; I grew up living a fallen life, with a fallen nature, in a fallen world system that I wasn't created for - and I didn't know it.

Then one day I escaped through the exit Door of Jesus' Life....and wow!

Astonished

Have you read in the Old Testament how Daniel sat astonished for days at the vision God had given him (Daniel 8:27)? Well, when I returned home from my trip with the girls, I too sat astonished – *joyfully* astonished – at what I had seen and experienced of Jesus and the Trinity of God.

Jesus said, *"I am the Door [to God]; by Me if any [girl] enters in, [she] shall be saved"* (John 10:9). And when I stepped through *that* Royal Door, I stepped right into the Glorious Kingdom of God, even while I was still living in this world!

Thankfully, I didn't have a job at the time, because all I wanted to do now was commune with Jesus and read all about Him and our Heavenly Father and the Holy Spirit in the Bible.

And so that's what I did, *continually*. I spent a major part of my days reading God's Word and communing with Jesus. In fact, I ended up reading the entire Bible *three times* that first year.

And as I familiarized myself with the four Gospels (Matthew, Mark, Luke, and John), I learned that Jesus had entered His Ministry at thirty years of age in a very precise, three-step way - *nothing* about it was haphazard!

Step 1: Receiving God's Divine Approval

The first step commenced as Jesus was baptized by John the Baptist. When He came up out of the water, the Spirit of God descended on Him in the form of a dove, and a Voice from Heaven said, *"This is My Beloved Son, in Whom I am well-pleased."*

This was God the Father's Official Announcement to the world about Jesus' Identity as a Member of the Trinity of God, and as Israel's long-awaited Messiah (Whom Israel knew would be the Son of God). And by saying, *"in Whom I am well-pleased,"* God was announcing His *Divine Approval* of His Son!

Step 2: Overcoming the Power of Satan

The second step took place immediately thereafter, when the Spirit of God sent Him into the wilderness, where He fasted for forty days and forty nights.

At the end of those days, when He was famished and His physical strength was at its weakest point, then came the devil to try to get Him to sin (so that He would be under Satan's spiritual dominion and authority from then on).

But Jesus didn't sin! And the devil flew away.

Step 3: Making the Official Announcement

Now, having been introduced and approved by God, and having overcome all the power of the devil, Jesus is ready to go forth to fulfill His Divine Commission as our Savior.

And so He makes His way to His hometown, enters the synagogue on the Sabbath, and announces Who He is and why He is here on Earth.

And it was so beautiful the way He did it! As was His custom on the Sabbath, He took the lectern to read the Scriptures. Except *this* time, He opened to an Old Testament prophecy of the Messiah, Isaiah 61, and read it to the congregation:

> *"The Spirit of the Lord God is upon Me; because He has anointed Me to preach glad tidings [good news] unto the meek.*
>
> *He has sent Me to bind up the broken-hearted, to proclaim liberty to the captives, and the opening of the prison to them that are bound."*

Then He said to the people, *"This day is this Scripture fulfilled in your ears."* This was Jesus' Official Announcement that He was, in fact, Israel's long-awaited Messiah!

272

And I can still remember when I first read that, how Jesus identified Himself with what that prophecy in Isaiah 61 said that the Messiah would be doing for all of us:

How He would be going about 'setting the captives free' from the power of sin and the authority of Satan, as well as from the death-to-God bondage of our fallen natures and the spiritual prison of the Fall of Man.

And I remember how thrilled I was to see that in my Bible - because here *Jesus had done that for me!*

And He had also given me *"beauty for ashes, the oil of joy for mourning, the garment of praise for the spirit of heaviness"* – as that prophecy goes on to say He would.

And my heart soared as I identified with what that Isaiah 61 prophecy then goes on to describe in verse 10:

How the day would come when the born again Bride of Christ, in response to all that the Messiah had done, would joyfully exclaim in Her heart:

> *"I will greatly rejoice in the Lord,*
> *my soul shall be joyful in my God;*
>
> *for He has clothed me with the Garments of Salvation,*
> *He has covered me with the Robe of [His] Righteousness,*
>
> *as a bridegroom decketh himself with ornaments,*
> *and as a bride adorns herself with her jewels."*

~ *43* ~

A Royal Introduction

"And Jesus said to them, Search the Scriptures...
for these are they that tell of Me."

(Luke 1:70)

HAVE you ever wondered what Snow White and Sleeping Beauty's Prince Charmings were like? And where they came from? They were handsome, they rode in on a white horse, that's all we know.

Neither prince came with a letter of introduction stamped with his family's gold seal, or with a birth certificate declaring his royal status.

Nor did either one come with official papers charting his ancestral history and diagramming his royal family tree.

No, neither prince came with any of that.

But Jesus did!

He came elaborately introduced to us in the Bible, containing declarations of His Royal Identity as the Second Person of the Trinity of God; and with diagrams of His earthly family tree and ancestral history; and with visions and prophecies of Him by prophets, priests, and kings.

He also came with light and music! And angels! A bright new star glittered in the sky over His Birthplace, and angels appeared to the shepherds, singing and rejoicing and declaring His Royal Identity and Purpose for coming here (Luke 2:7-16).

That's how our Divine Prince Charming came to us! *That's* how respectfully and honorably our Prince of Life approached us!

And *that's* what I saw revealed of Him in the Bible after I met Him and was filled with His Life! Along with the revelation of our Heavenly Father and the Holy Spirit in those Sacred Pages, I saw the Glorious Son of God shining through from Genesis to Revelation!

Glittering

I haven't shared this with you yet, but I had been raised in a religion that not only denies the Trinity of God and the Deity of Jesus, but one that has a bad habit of taking Bible verses out of context to prove its heretical doctrine.

Now, however, having seen the Living God for myself, I loved seeing Jesus' Deity revealed in the Bible, not only in the New Testament, but the Old Testament as well.

In fact, as the ocean sparkles on a sunny day, I saw the Old Testament literally *glittering* from beginning to end with prophecies of Jesus as our Lord and Savior.

As John the Baptist's father, a high priest, told the people, Jesus had been prophesied of *"since the world began"* (Luke 1:70).

And Jesus confirmed John's word about this several times. For example, one day when the Pharisees were confronting Him yet again about His Identity, He said to them: *"Search the Scriptures...for these are they that tell of Me"* (John 5:39).

Later, after His Death and Resurrection, He confirmed John's word again when He appeared to the two grieving men as they were walking on the road to Emmaus.

They had believed Him to be the Messiah, but now He was gone, and they were perplexed about why He'd died. *"Couldn't He Who had commanded the wind and walked on the water have prevented the soldiers from crucifying Him?"* they reasoned together.

And as they were walking along, lamenting the Lord's Death, He came alongside them in the form of a fellow traveler and asked them why they were so sad.

And after they told Him why, He comforted them by explaining the purpose for the Messiah's Death: *"Beginning at Moses and all the prophets, He expounded to them in all the Scriptures the things concerning Himself"* (Luke 24:27).

(Wouldn't you like to have heard *that*!?)

277

And then there was Peter. After Pentecost, when God was extending Salvation to the Gentiles, Peter said to Cornelius the Gentile:

> *"To [Jesus],* **all the prophets** *give witness that,*
> *through His Name, whosoever believes in Him*
> *shall receive forgiveness of sins."*

(Acts 10:43)

Out of the Mouth of Babes....and God

But it wasn't just "all the prophets" that foretold of Jesus! Psalmists, kings, priests, and ordinary Old Testament people did as well.

As did God Himself! Our Heavenly Father spent centuries prophesying of His Son as our Lord and Savior; not only through the prophets, but through His Laws and Commandments, Precepts and Promises, and in one way or another through the lives of the patriarchs of old.

God also prophesied of Jesus as our Lord and Savior, and of His Life as our Royal Clothing through:

* The architectural layout of the Temple

* The interior furnishings

* The garments worn by the priests

* The blood of the spotless lambs and rams sacrificed for the atonement of sin.

278

Oh, how patiently and perfectly God went before His Son over the centuries, laying the prophetic groundwork for the revelation of Him in Person!

And, oh, our *lavish* God - He also encrypted prophecies of the Life of Jesus as our Royal Clothing into many (if not most) of the Old Testament stories as well! So many, in fact, that I'd love to go off the rails right now and chronicle them all for you right here!

But how about I restrain myself, and in the next chapter share a short but sweet overview of just two instead? So you can see what I'm talking about?

Sound good? Okay, here they are - I think you're going to love them as I do!

~ 44 ~

Jesus and Our Royal Clothing Foretold

"Open my eyes, Lord God, that I might behold
wondrous things out of Thy Word."

(Psalm 119:18)

REVELATION 19:10 says, *"The testimony of Jesus is the spirit of prophecy."* And this is what we see of Jesus in the Old Testament!

Unlike the fortune-telling that is so prevalent in the world today, God teaches us in His Word that true prophecy comes from Him and involves the testimony of Jesus and what He is going to do in our lives, or in the world per se.

And this is what we see in the following two prophecies I want to share with you. The first involves an interaction between Elijah and Elisha. And the second is about the Branch of the Tree of Life that extends down to us from Paradise in Heaven.

281

The First Prophecy: Elijah and Elisha

I love this prophecy! As it happened, one day Elijah (that super-anointed prophet and priest of God) was led by God to cast his coat on an Israelite farmer named Elisha as he was plowing his field with twelve oxen (First Kings 19:19).

Now, if someone did that to us today, we might think it weird. But Elisha understood exactly what that coat meant!

Throughout Israel's history, the act of 'putting on' clothing by the leading of the Holy Spirit in certain instances was a sign of God interacting in, or speaking into, a given situation.

Now, whether God spoke directly to Elisha's mind about the meaning of the coat, or he had the Witness of the Holy Spirit that came with it, Elisha knew that he had just been called by God to serve Him alongside Elijah.

"And so he arose...and went after Elijah..." (First Kings 19:21).

But get this: *Elisha didn't go until he had first burned his proverbial bridges behind him!*

Taking his calling of God seriously, Elisha slew his oxen and made a fire of their wooden yokes (yokes are those contraptions farmers used to place around an oxen's neck so it could pull the plow).

Then Elisha cooked the meat of the oxen on the fire and gave it to his family and friends.

And then he followed Elijah!

282

In other words, by giving up his means of earning a living (the yokes and his oxen to plow the fields), Elisha made no provision for himself to come back to his old life.

And that's a prophecy of us with Jesus: When we're finally, truly *done* with the emptiness of this fallen world, and more than ready to exchange our fallen nature for the Life and Nature of Jesus, we're not messing around.

We're not simply joining a church and saying, 'Voila, now I'm a born again Christian.' Neither are we stashing a little of our old nature in some secret life-tent for safekeeping, just in case we change our mind and want to go back to our old life.

No, we're not 'trying' Jesus to see if we like walking with Him, as if He's some spiritual car we can take for a test spin around the block to see if we want to keep Him.

No, coming to Jesus is not a game with us. We're serious. We're all in. So we look up (or get on our knees), and with all of our heart and mind and soul invite Him into our lives as our Lord and Savior.

And seeing our heart, Jesus joyfully responds by clothing us with His Divine Life (prophesied of by Elijah placing his coat on Elisha), and we happily enter our New Life with Him!

The Second Prophecy – The BRANCH

This prophecy is short and sweet, but *awesome.* And obviously God thinks so too, because He repeated it *five times* in the Old Testament!

Once in Isaiah, twice in Jeremiah, and twice in Zechariah (Isaiah 11:1-10; Jeremiah 23:5-6; 33:15; Zechariah 3:1-9; 6:12-13).

The prophecy is about Jesus' Life as the "BRANCH" of the "Tree of Life" extending down to us from Heaven's Paradise, where the Throne of God is located (Rev. 2:7; 22:14).

We get our first glimpse of this Tree at the beginning of the Bible, where the "Tree of Life" stood in the midst of the Garden of Eden (from which, before the Fall, God had invited Adam and Eve to eat freely - Genesis 2:9).

Then, at the *end* of the Bible, we see this Tree of Life again; only this time it's shown to us as located in the midst of "Paradise" in Heaven (Revelation 2:7).

In between these references, however, in the *middle* of the Bible, God prophesies *five times* about Jesus' Life as the "BRANCH" of this Tree of Life extending down to us from Heaven's Paradise.

Let me show you just one of God's prophecies from the five I listed above - Zechariah 3:1-9.

In this prophecy, Joshua, a high priest, was lifted into the presence of "the angel of the Lord" (meaning, into the Presence of the Lord God Himself).

And there, as the priestly representative of Israel, Joshua's "filthy garments" were removed from him, and he was clothed with new, clean garments. Then God said to Joshua:

"Hear now, O Joshua...for behold, I will bring forth My Servant, the BRANCH" (verse 8). And then God told him that by this Branch, He would remove the sin of the land *"in one day"* (verse 9).

And that's what Jesus did! He dealt with the sin of the world *in one day.* He was crucified in the morning, and He died before the sun went down.

And the *"land"* referred to in that prophecy was Jerusalem. And Jesus was crucified in Jerusalem; He rose from the dead in Jerusalem; and Pentecost happened in Jerusalem.

And from Jerusalem, the Gospel of Christ has gone out to the whole world, and people's sins are removed when they are born again. And that's what the "filthy garments" that were removed from Joshua depicted.

And the new, clean clothing placed on Joshua prophesied of the Royal Clothing of Jesus' Holy Life that our souls would be born again with when we believe in Him as our Savior.

And I love that the thief on the cross next to Jesus said, *"Lord, remember me when you come into your Kingdom"* (Luke 23:42). And Jesus said to him, *"Truly, I say unto you, Today, you shall be with me in Paradise."*

The Breath of Life

And there they are, dearly Beloved of God – two wonderful prophecies of Jesus and His Life as our Royal Clothing! There are

285

many more, as I said. And while some are easily spotted, others are encrypted, and at least in my case required the Holy Spirit's illumination to help me see them.

Makes me think of the movie *National Treasure*. If you've seen it, you'll recall that two of the main characters - a treasure hunter and a professional art restorer - applied a dab of lemon juice to the upper right corner of the back of the Declaration of Independence, and then they gently breathed on it.

When the lemon juice reacted with the heat of their breath, an encrypted code within the parchment appeared, and with that code they were able to find the hidden treasure.

And that's like the prophecies of Jesus in the Old Testament: When the Breath of God through the Holy Spirit fills us with His Life, our spiritual eyes are opened.

And not only can we then see more clearly and understand more comprehensively the overt prophecies of Jesus and our Royal Clothing, but as we continue to look, the Holy Spirit helps us discern the many more encrypted into the text.

Altogether they weave a Royal Tapestry of our King, literarily woven in gold, red, blue, and purple: Gold representing His Deity as the Son of God. Red representing the Sacrifice of His Holy Blood as our Savior. Blue representing His Heavenly Nature and Character. Purple representing His Divine Royalty as the *King of kings and Lord of lords!*

~ 45 ~

The Way, the Truth, and the Life

"And [I saw] above the firmament...the likeness of a throne,
like a sapphire stone: and on the throne was the
appearance of a Man,

and downward, round about the throne, was the appearance
of fire, so bright was its shining.
And above and around the throne was the appearance
of a rainbow.

This was the appearance of the likeness of the Glory of the Lord.
And when I saw it, I fell on my face..."

(Ezekiel 1:26-28)

DO you remember those rainbows depicted in our childhood storybooks? The kind with a pot of gold at the end? Well, after I met Jesus, I discovered the quintessential of that rainbow and its gold in the Bible!

The Rainbow is Jesus, and the Gold is His Life - *God's Riches in Glory given to us in Christ Jesus* (John 17:22; Ephesians 1:3).

Jesus is our Treasure and Exceeding Great Reward when we put our faith in Him as our Lord and Savior (Genesis 15:1; Second Corinthians 4:7; Ephesians chapters 1 & 2).

And like a Divine Rainbow, the overarching Truth of the Bible from Genesis to Revelation was revealed by Him when He said to the people: *"I am the Way, the Truth, and the Life..."* (John 14:6). Expansively, He was saying:

I AM THE WAY

for you to be born into the Kingdom of God and walk
in Divine Power, Victory, and Blessing

I AM THE TRUTH

the Personification of the Trinity of God, the God of
Truth, Who exists and loves you; and by My Life you can
know and walk in the Light of God's Truth, rather than in
the lies of the world, the flesh, and the devil

I AM THE LIFE

of God manifested to you, so that by receiving My Life,
you can live in Oneness with Me and with all of Heaven's
Royalty, now, here on Earth, and forever in the Kingdom
of God.

Now, I ask you, can it get any better or sweeter than that? I mean, at the same time Jesus is telling us *Who He is*, He's also telling us *Who He is FOR US*!

And you know, I can't help but think of the contrast between Him and that selfish emperor in the fable '*The Emperor's New Clothes.*'

The Emperor's New Clothes

You probably know this fable already, but for those who don't, it's about an emperor who wanted to be like a god in the eyes of the people of his realm. Not satisfied with being esteemed as just an *emperor*, he wanted to be worshipped as deity – as a god.

Well, after consulting with his advisors on this, they all decided that the best way for him to accomplish such a feat was to be more exquisitely and richly dressed than everyone else.

So he commanded his staff designers to make over-the-top outfits for him, unlike any the world had ever seen.

And they did! They rose to the challenge, called forth their most creative imaginations and made many fantastic outfits, each woven of gold, silver, and colorful threads, and adorned with costly jewels.

And the emperor was very pleased! He loved his new clothes, and each day he looked forward to wearing the next outfit, and then the next and the next and the next.....until, finally, the inevitable happened: The designers' creativity became exhausted and they ran out of new ideas.

So he fired them and hired some new designers.

But eventually the same thing happened. As talented as these new fashionistas were at making stunning outfits for him, their creativity also had limits, and in time they too ran out of new ideas.

And this wasn't fun for them, because the more they couldn't satisfy the emperor's desire for out-of-this-world clothing, the more he berated them, and even threatened their lives.

So they tricked him. They told him that they were designing a '*new*' kind of outfit for him; one so incredible, he wouldn't even be able to *see* it. Only those *below* his status could see it, they explained, because 'his eyes were too lofty, too royal, too *divine* to see it.' (Snicker, snicker.)

Now, at first, the emperor didn't know what to think. The idea of 'invisible' clothing seemed preposterous to him. But the wily designers feigned such excitement as they went about creating his 'absolutely divine' new outfit, that eventually he fell for their trick and believed them.

And when they saw this, then they really played it up! Faking great enthusiasm whenever he was within earshot, they 'gushed' loudly over the invisible outfit as they 'worked' on it each day, and they talked about how the people of his realm would finally see him as a god.

And their subterfuge worked! The emperor was finally inspired to such great heights of imagination that he ordered a special event to be planned in his honor. A grand day when he would present himself to his kingdom wearing his glorious new threads!

Steppin' Out in Style

Royal invitations, gold-edged and embossed, were sent out to all the people. And royal messengers traveled throughout the province, heralding the great event. Soon all the realm was waiting with abated breath to see 'THE EMPEROR'S NEW CLOTHES.'

And when that day came and the designers 'clothed' the emperor with his new outfit, he paraded out before all the people with great pomp and circumstance. Stark naked. And after a collective gasp, the people laughed at him and made fun of his body.

Humility Comes Before Honor

Proverbs 16:18 says, *"Pride goeth before destruction, and a haughty spirit before a fall."* And that's what happened to this selfish emperor!

Not satisfied with being the ruler over, like, *everything,* he desired personal exaltation beyond that which is given to mere mortals. Elevating his people and making provisions for them to be clothed better was not his bag. All he wanted was glory and honor for himself.

Now, in contrast, look at what Philippians 2:5-8 says about Jesus:

"Let this mind be in you, which was also in Christ Jesus:

Who, being in the form of God, thought it not robbery to be equal with God, but made Himself of no reputation,

and took upon Himself the form of a servant, made in the likeness of men.

And being found in fashion as a man, He humbled Himself, and became obedient unto death, even the death of the Cross."

There He was, the *real* King of the universe! But unlike that selfish emperor intent on exalting himself over his people, Jesus set aside His Royal Robes in Glory, came here as a Man, let the soldiers strip Him of the one earthly robe He did have, and then He let them beat Him to a pulp and hang Him on a Cross.

All so that *we* could be dressed better! All so that *we* could have the opportunity to lay aside the rags of our old fallen nature and be clothed upon with the Glory of His Divine Life and Nature!

"Therefore, God has highly exalted Him, and given Him a Name which is above every name:

that at the Name of Jesus every knee should bow, in Heaven, on earth, and under the earth;

and that every tongue should confess that Jesus Christ is Lord, to the Glory of God the Father."

(Philippians 2:9-11)

292

~ 46 ~

You Shall Know the Truth

And Jesus said, "You shall know [Me] the Truth,
and [I] the Truth shall make you free."

(John 8:32)

WHENEVER I think of what Jesus went through to clothe us with His Life, I want to kiss His nail-scarred Hands and Feet, look deeply into His Eyes and tell Him how grateful I am.

The fact that He so wanted you and me and everyone to *know* Him and be *with* Him in God the Father's Presence throughout eternity, that He gave Himself over to the lictors to be scourged and crucified to make it possible astounds me!

He is God's Living Word of Life - *the Truth of all there is and behind all there is* manifested to us from Heaven, and yet He did all that for us!

Honestly, though, before I met Jesus, I'm not sure I could have understood such a seeming anomaly as a PERSON being 'THE TRUTH OF ALL THERE IS.'

Knowing how my mind works, I would have considered '*the Truth of all there is*' to be a series of facts put together – empirical evidence of this, that, and the other.

But when I met Jesus, then I understood. And to illustrate how, imagine I said to you, "I love you." *That* truth - the truth of my love for you – that would not be something you could see or touch, right?

Only by my complimentary, non-critical words, and by my kind, respectful, loving actions toward you, as well as by the amiable way I looked at you, smiled at you, etc., could you comprehend my love.

So even though you couldn't see or touch the non-physical *truth* of my love for you, you could see and touch *me* - the *personification* of it!

The Personification of Truth

And that's like Jesus: He is the *Personification* of the Trinity of God –"*the God of Truth*" (Psalm 31:5; John 1:1-14; 17:17).

And He came down to us from Heaven as a *Person*, and the people *saw* Him and *heard* Him and *touched* Him.

As His disciple, John, wrote (and I'll shorten it):

> *"That which was from the Beginning [Jesus],*
> *Whom we have **heard** and **seen** and **touched**,*

Oh, I know it doesn't always *seem* like we are 'set free' from our fallen nature when we're born again. But we must understand, it's our *soul* (our Me, Myself, and I within our bodies) that is set free.

Our old fallen nature was kicked out of our soul when it was replaced by the Life and Nature of Jesus when we were born again.

It's just that *our physicality* is still part of this fallen world (you know, ashes-to-ashes, dust-to-dust, and all).

And our physical brain is still programmed with all that we saw, heard, learned, and experienced while living in this world with a fallen nature.

And God has ordained it this way! Because now, as born again Believers, we have a Glorious Destiny ahead of us, one of ruling and reigning with Jesus throughout eternity as His Bride.

And that 'ruling and reigning' part comes with major responsibility! For to think with the Mind of Christ and to be like Him as His Bride is no small feat! Therefore, God has us in Royal Training by the Holy Spirit to prepare us for that important Destiny!

And so a large part of the Holy Spirit's Royal Curriculum is to teach us how to *think* with the Mind of Christ according to the Word of God in order to Divinely *renew* and *regroove* our physical brain with God's Truth.

And as we do that, we not only bring our minds but also our physical bodies into subjection to our soul's New Life and Nature in Christ (First Corinthians 9:27; Second Corinthians 10:5)!

Royal Training

Of course, all this would be much easier if there weren't demonic forces trying to prevent it!

Evil spirits know that we are in Royal Training for our Glorious Destiny of ruling and reigning with Christ. And so they go about trying to sabotage our Training, most often by a few well-worn tactics.

Tactics like inserting lies and other thoughts into our minds that are not our own; flashing evil images into our minds; bringing up hurtful memories, stirring up our physical bodies with inordinate desires, etc.

All with the end game of grieving us, confusing us, making us angry, and provoking us to sin; anything to hinder us from manifesting the Life and Love of Jesus through our mortal bodies in this world.

And these tactics are nothing new to Satan's arsenal! Over two thousand years ago, that devil worked behind the scenes, provoking those who crucified Christ. Satan obviously wanted to get Jesus out of this world so that His Life wouldn't continue to be manifested to the people.

And now Satan is trying to do the same thing to us!

Through an army of evil spirits, Satan tries to keep Jesus from being manifested to the world through the born again Believer's physicality. And so Satan orders his evil spirits to hassle our physical minds and bodies through all those above-mentioned tactics.

But no worries, God has it all under control! It's all part of our Royal Training. Whether we're aware of it or not, the Holy Spirit is continually teaching us how to walk in and manifest Jesus' Life – a Divine and very *Royal* Life through which we have undefeatable Victory over 'the world, the flesh, and the devil.'

And we're going to ace our Royal Training; because as Romans 8:37 tells us, *"we are more than conquerors through Him that loved us* [so much that He would die for us]."

Just as in the Old Covenant, it was up to human effort to fulfill God's requirements for holiness (and the best human efforts failed), now, in the New Covenant, it is accomplished by the *Life of Christ in us.*

As Jesus said to the Pharisees, *"Think not that I've come to destroy the Law or the prophets; I am not come to destroy, but to **fulfill"** (Matthew 5:17).

And this is where we come back around to the seven facets of the Armor of God – the *Breastplate of Righteousness* being the second facet; for it is Jesus' Righteousness *in us* that is our Righteousness before God.

As we've seen, the Armor of God is a Divine Pattern of the Life of Christ within us. And spelling it out for us in seven facets, God has revealed how we can walk in the Life of Christ within us and manifest Him through our mortal bodies in this world.

So we must not think of these seven facets simply as 'tools' that we can pick up and use against the enemy, and then put down and go on our way. They are the Life of Jesus *in us* empowering us over all the tactics of the enemy; as well as delivering us in our trials, making a way for us where there is no way, being our Savior and Provider in every situation.

You get the point: The mystery of Godliness is *Christ in you* (Colossians 1:26-27). And our Royal Training is designed by God to teach us to walk with Jesus in *His Power* and in *Oneness with Him* as our Righteousness, our Shield, our Sword, our Helmet, our Shoes of Peace, *our very Life!*

Set Up to Win

And oh, *the Riches of the Glory we have in Christ*, even when we fail our Royal Training on any given day; because His Holy Blood continually *cleanses us of all sin* (First John 1:7,9).

And as an added measure of Divine Protection, *"There is no condemnation to those who are in Christ Jesus...for the law of the Spirit of life in Christ **has made me free** from the law of sin and death"* (Romans 8:1-2).

The "law of sin and death" means 'you sin, you die to God.' But Jesus' Life within us has **set us free** from that law!

Oh, I know there are those who point to the last part of verse 1 (which I didn't include in the above quote, but I'll show you in a minute), thinking to prove that our position of 'no condemnation' by God is 'conditional' upon our 'behavior.' But they're not applying verse 9 to the text.

302

Let me show you what I mean. Let's look at the fullness of verses 1 and 2, with verse 9 inserted in between, so you can see what I'm talking about:

> Verse 1: *"There is therefore now no condemnation to those who are in Christ Jesus, **who walk not after the flesh**, but after the Spirit."*

> Verse 9: *"But you are **not in the flesh** if so be the Spirit of God dwells in you."*

> Verse 2: *"For the law of the Spirit of Life in Christ Jesus has made me free from the law of sin and death."*

See that? When verse 1 refers to those *"who walk not after the flesh,"* it's not using the word 'walk' to denote the way we behave.

It's not the transliteration of the word 'walk' used in other verses that specifically address the way we act – like Ephesians 5:2, for example, which says: *"Walk in love, as Christ also has loved us, and has given Himself for us..."*

In that verse, the root form of the word 'walk' – *walk in love* – denotes how we act or behave toward others.

But not so in Romans 8:1 where it says, *"There is no condemnation to those who walk not after the flesh but after the Spirit..."* The root form of *that* word *"walk"* there refers to the *life-source* of the born again Believer's soul!

Which is, in fact, the Life of Christ, *not* our old fallen nature (referred to there as the *"flesh")*.

So what the opening of Romans 8 is *really* saying is this: '*There is therefore no condemnation to those who are in Christ Jesus, whose life-source does not consist of the old fallen nature, but rather of the Life and Nature of Christ.*'

Which means we are free to go through our Royal Training without being rejected by God when we stumble and fail it by not acting out perfect behavior on any given day!

Just as we wouldn't reject our little child from our family if she kept falling down when trying to learn to walk, but rather we would give her all the more help and training, so God doesn't reject us when we fail our Royal Training.

Instead, the more we fail, the more assistance He gives us through the Holy Spirit!

And this is what I and others like me have experienced over decades of walking with Jesus. He has been gentle and patient with us in our failings, forgiving us, strengthening us, delivering us, and working within us, first to will and then to do of His Good Pleasure as One Who is *Love*.

Jesus is our Good Shepherd, and He gently, wisely, lovingly leads us onwards and upwards in paths of Victory, rather than condemning us and throwing us away when we fail. He paid a high price to bring us out of the darkness of the Fall of Man into His marvelous Light, and He will never leave us nor forsake us.

Which is, in fact, what 'circumcision' in the Old Testament was all about!

Circumcision

As you probably know, circumcision is the cutting away of the physical foreskin that covers a man's (ahem) place that makes babies.

And God instituted circumcision in Genesis 17:10-11 as a prophecy of how His Holy Son Jesus would come here one day and provide the way for our souls to be set free from the death-to-God consequences of the Fall of Man by giving us His Life.

For not only is the Fall of Man a death-shroud that keeps our soul entombed from God, but it also keeps our mind and heart imprisoned in spiritual darkness and hides the beauty of our True Identity.

But when we are born again, that death-shroud is immediately removed from our soul, circumcised by God "*by the circumcision made without [physical] hands*" (Colossians 2:11), and our soul is set free from our fallen nature, as well as from the death-to-God consequences of sin and the spiritual darkness of the Fall of Man.

Which, not coincidentally, is what Jesus' parable of a seed was all about!

The Parable of a Seed

Anyone who gardens understands the life-out-of-death process of a seed. A seed is entombed by its outer husk, and unless that husk dies and is shed, the seed inside cannot sprout and grow. It simply remains inactive – alive, but encased in its own tomb.

But when the seed is planted in the darkness of dirt and watered each day, eventually its outer husk withers, splits open and dies, and the life of the seed is set free to sprout into the light.

And this is what Jesus was prophetically referring to in His parable of a seed in John 12:24-25, where He said:

> *"Truly, truly, I say unto you, except a corn of wheat falls into the ground and dies, it abides alone: but if it dies, it brings forth much fruit."*

Before Jesus shared that parable, He had been exhorting the people not to cling to their fallen lives, but rather to follow Him. And we now understand that "following Him" means replacing our fallen life with His Divine Life.

And when we do, then our beautiful souls are set free to live in the Divine Light of *Oneness* with Him, and with all of Heaven's Royalty!

Just as He prayed for in the Garden of Gethsemane, saying:

> *"[Father, I pray] that they may be One in Us;*
> *as You, Father, are in Me, and I in You,*
>
> *[so I pray] that they also may be One in Us...*
> *and the Glory You have given Me, I am giving them;*
>
> *that they may be One in Us, even as We are One...*
> *for You have loved them as You have loved Me..."*

(John 17:21-23)

306

Oh, dearly Beloved of God, many a great treasure has traveled many a distant land and sea, all to be laid at the feet of many a beloved bride. But none can compare to the Matchless Gift of *Oneness with Heaven's Royalty* bestowed upon us by our Savior Bridegroom - the *"King of Glory"* (Psalm 24:1, 7-9; John 17:24).

He left the splendor of Heaven, traversed the Pleiades and galaxies of planets and distant stars, walked on the wings of the wind, split the atom to come here as the Son of Man possessing the DNA of Holy God. And then He laid down His Life to conquer Hell's fire on our behalf!

All to lay at our feet His *'Riches in Glory'* and make us *One* with Himself (Ephesians 1:18); now to be *"Child of God the Father, Bride of the Eternal Son, Dwelling-Place of God the Spirit, thus with Christ made ever One"* (Gerhard Tersteegen).

~ 48 ~

The King and Us

And Jesus prayed, "Father, I will that they also,
whom you have given Me, be with Me where I am..."

(John 17:24)

WELL, here we are - we've come full circle looking at the correlation between our Royal Story and the plotlines in *Snow White* and *Sleeping Beauty*!

To briefly recap, first we saw that just as their stories open with the revelation of their royal identity, so does ours. The Bible reveals in its very opening chapter that we were created in the Image and Likeness of Heaven's Royalty.

Then we saw that just as those lovely princesses were tricked by evil into a state of sleeping death, so were we - tricked by evil Satan into a lower nature, and thereby into a state of spiritual death-to-God through the Fall.

And, finally, we saw that just as they each had a prince charming who came along on a white horse to save them, so do we.

But ours isn't any ol' prince of a province! Ours is *JESUS*, the "Prince of Life" Himself (Acts 3:15; 5:31) - THE KING OF KINGS AND LORD OF LORDS!

*"And I saw Heaven opened, and behold, **a white horse**, and He that sat on him was called Faithful and True...*

And He was clothed with a vesture dipped in [His own] Blood: and His Name is called The Word of God.

And on His Vesture and on His Thigh, His Name was written: 'KING OF KINGS AND LORD OF LORDS.' "

(Revelation 19:11, 13, 16)

Jesus is also called *"The Prince of princes"* in Daniel 8:25; *"Messiah the Prince"* in Daniel 9:25; *"The Prince of Peace"* in Isaiah 9:6; and *"The Prince of the kings of the Earth"* in Revelation 1:5.

And just as Snow White and Sleeping Beauty were awakened by the kiss of true love, and the moment their eyes opened they looked into their prince's face and fell in love with him, that's what we see of Jesus and us in 'The Song of Solomon' in the Old Testament!

You know how some couples adopt a particular song as *their* song? The one they were dancing to when they fell in love? Perhaps the one playing when they first kissed?

310

Well, 'The Song of Solomon' is our Song with Jesus. It's a Heavenly Love Song revealing the Divine and *very Holy* Love Relationship between Heaven's Bride and Bridegroom while She is still here in this world.

And after its introduction in verse one, the Song officially opens in verse two with the newly born again Bride of Christ exclaiming joyfully:

"Let Him kiss me with the kisses of His Mouth,
for [His] Love is better than wine!"

And the first time I read that after I was born again, everything in me said, *'Yes! That's how I felt when I met Jesus! And how I still feel! His Presence and the Words of His Mouth are like pure, Holy Kisses of God's Love to my soul!'*

The Word of God, the Word of Love

As the Image and Fullness of the invisible God, Jesus is 'the Living Word of God' manifested to us. As John 1:1-2 & 14 tells us:

"In the beginning was the Word,
and the Word was with God,
and the Word was God.
The same was in the beginning with God.

And the Word [Jesus] was made flesh and dwelt among us,
and we beheld His Glory, the Glory as of the Only Begotten
of the Father, full of Grace and Truth."

311

In those verses, we learn that Jesus is the **Word of God Manifested to us in Person**.

And God is *Love,* therefore the Presence of Jesus and the Words that He speaks to us feel like *pure, Holy Kisses of God's Love to our souls!*

And so the heart of the newly born again Bride of Christ exclaims, *'Let Him, O my soul! Let Him kiss me with the Love of God spoken by the Sweetness of His Mouth; for never did wine make me feel so happy and consoled!'*

And oh, that Jesus is willing to step into our space and lift us to God is mercifully kind; for we don't have the power to raise ourselves from the death-to-God effects of the Fall of Man.

Just as Snow White and Sleeping Beauty could not awaken or raise themselves from their sleeping death, neither can we. We need Jesus, the Prince of Life, to do that for us.

Choosing Jesus

But there's an important distinction here between our Royal Story and the plotlines of those beloved fairytales. For it was *after* Snow White and Sleeping Beauty were raised from their sleeping death that they got to choose to embrace their prince and become his royal bride.

Whereas in real life, we must make our choice *beforehand - by faith*. As Ephesians 2:8 says: *"By God's Grace are you saved through faith [in Jesus]..."*

Regardless of what happened to us (all Mankind) in the Fall, we are still awake in our sleeping death-to-God, and we still have a free will and the power to choose for ourselves.

And when we *do* actually choose to open our hearts to Jesus, embrace Him by faith as our Lord and Savior and receive His Life, then 'Positionally' speaking, we are *"in Christ"* (Ephesians 1:1,13).

And where is Jesus - Positionally speaking? *At the Right Hand of God the Father* (Hebrews 1:3). That is His 'Position' in the Kingdom of God!

So again, where are we as those who are *"in Christ"*? We are exactly where Ephesians 2:6 tells us we are - *seated together with Christ in Heavenly Places! That* is our 'Position' in the Kingdom of God as those who have received Jesus' Life and become One with Heaven's Royalty!

Which means, 'Positionally' speaking, *our souls are already living in the Castle in the Kingdom of God!*

And just as Jesus is seated at the Right Hand of God, and yet He is here with us always (as His very Name *'Immanuel'* means, "God *with* us"), so we are seated with Him in Heavenly Places, even while we're still here in this world! As Ephesians 2:4-6 says:

"For God, Who is rich in Mercy, for His great Love wherewith He loved us, has quickened us together with Christ (for by Grace are you saved); and has raised us up together, and made us sit together in Heavenly Places in Christ Jesus."

313

Which means (drum roll, please), *we are abiding in Christ!*

Abiding in Christ

You know how Jesus said to His disciples at the Last Supper, *"Abide in Me, and I will abide in you"* (John 15:4)?

Well, not only was He going to die on the Cross the next day to make such 'abiding' possible, but He was prophetically exhorting His disciples – and all of us - to receive His Divine Life by being born again after He rose from the dead and sent it down to us on the Day of Pentecost.

For, you see, the word 'abide' is not a verb (an action word). Rather, Webster's Dictionary defines it as *"to live in – in a fixed state."*

Same with Roget's Thesaurus - it connects the word 'abide' to the synonyms *"live, dwell, reside."*

In other words, when Jesus said, *"Abide in Me, and I will abide in you,"* He was not telling us to get on a treadmill of unceasing good behavior to maintain a Life-Connection to Him.

Rather, He was exhorting us to make His Life our soul's Divine Residence by being born again after He made it available to us!

And when we do, then we are *abiding* [living, residing] *in Him*, and He is *abiding* [living, residing] *in us*, in a fixed, non-fluctuating state of being!

314

Just as Colossians 1:13 says of us when we receive Jesus' Life, *"God has delivered us from the power of darkness and has translated our souls into the Kingdom of His dear Son."*

And I remember as a little girl looking with fascination at that last scene in the fairytales, where each princess rides off with her handsome prince on his white horse, a golden image of his castle glimmering in the distance ahead of them. And I remember feeling so happy about it. And now I know why:

Because in that final scene, the Holy Spirit was witnessing to my young heart the Beautiful, Divine Love Story of Heaven's Bride and Bridegroom - a 'Dream Come True' that Jesus has made possible for all of us to enter into and live 'Happily Ever After' in Oneness with Him, and with all of Heaven's Royalty, now and forever in the Kingdom of God!

"And the Spirit and the Bride say, 'Come...'
And let them who are thirsty come.
And whosoever will, let them take
of the Water of Life freely."

(Revelation 22:17)

Epilogue

IT'S hard to say goodbye. So let's not and go to lunch in Monte Carlo instead. (Literarily speaking.) That's the geographical area where God once gave me a sort of vision of the Bride of Christ arrayed in her Royal Wedding Clothing, ascending to the Throne of God for the Marriage Supper of the Lamb, and I'd like to share it with you here.

First, though, I want to say that this vision was *not* the *real* thing. I mean, considering the number of people that have been born again since Pentecost (over *two-thousand years* ago), I think it's safe to assume that there will be billions of born again Believers joining Jesus at the Marriage Supper. Wouldn't you say?

And what I saw in this vision was not *that*. Rather, as I understand it, the vision was given to me as a visual aid to support me in writing this book (which I was in the middle of outlining at the time).

And to say the least, it was a *lovely* visual aid; one that contrasted the difference between the earthly clothing we put on our physical bodies, and the Divine (and very *Royal)* Clothing that Jesus gives us of His Life. And it will be my joy to share with you what I saw.

So let's go now to Monte Carlo, where it all began.

The Opulent City

Monte Carlo, as you may know, is the only official 'city' in the country of Monaco, which is a small but opulent principality that sits on the Mediterranean Sea between France and Italy.

You may also know that the American actress, Grace Kelly, married Prince Rainier of Monaco back in the late 1950's, and subsequently they raised their three children in the royal palace situated on a bluff across the bay from the Monte Carlo Casino.

Well, as it happened, one morning my sister, Pam, and I were drinking coffee on the patio of her timeshare condo on the French Riviera. And seeing that the sky was clear and bright blue, the day seemed perfect for a drive along the coastline, so we decided to have lunch in Monte Carlo.

It was early spring. Some places in the world were still as gray as a northern horizon in winter, and colder. In other places, the moon was still cutting into midnight.

But on our side of the world, on the warm Mediterranean, spring had already sprouted wings and called all seedling-dreamers to awake from their earthen hibernation, rise from their blankets of cozy husks, and set the world agog with their blossoms.

They twitched awake in their little seedling beds, sent up a few green shoots to test the weather, and by the time Pam and I had put on our finest daywear and begun our two-hour trip to Monte Carlo, they had already burst forth into the sunlight and were paying homage to our Elegant Creator by reflecting His Beauty.

Enchantment

A seed is a small thing. It can easily be blown from the palm of your hand with nothing more than a puff of breath, yet we feed on its increase and live by its culture. Of it, we demand our most basic needs for sustenance, for beauty, for inspiration.

And as Pam drove expertly along the coastline and I enjoyed the view from the passenger seat, both beauty and inspiration were abundantly available. In less than an hour, the road we were on climbed higher and higher until we found ourselves skirting the precipice of a mountain, hundreds of feet above the ocean, dancing with hot sparkles of morning sunlight.

I can't properly describe the color of the water; to say the least it was a combination of royal blue and ultramarine blue, and artistically I was shocked by it. Never had I seen such a blue.

And apparently neither had the French impressionist painter, Monet. While visiting this same area of the Mediterranean in 1884, he wrote to his sister that he was "stunned" by the "alarming brilliance" of the water's blue hue, and that he was "appalled" at the colors that his paint palette offered as he tried to capture it on canvas.

As for me, immediately I saw the water, I wanted to reach out to it, dive into it, roll around in its glorious hue.

321

And it wasn't just me feeling that way, soon the mountain beneath us began extending massive earthen arms out to the sea, as if trying to hug the gorgeous water, but not quite getting its hands together.

Again and again as we drove along, the mountain beneath us reached out to the sea. And each time it failed to get its hands together, it created yet another tranquil bay for yachts and sailboats to enter, put down anchor and go to sleep, while their owners basked in the sun and played in the water.

Words fail me here to describe the exquisite beauty of the scenery as we navigated the precipice of the mountain road, listening to the music of Abba. I loved how each bay far below us was edged with fabulous sprawling estates surrounded by vast green lawns and lots of palm trees, and how there were also lavish boutique hotels tucked under lines of even more palm trees.

Also, I loved how the emerald greens of the grass and foliage complimented the blue of the water, and how the white of the boats glinted here and there with sunlight, as if part of it.

Mesmerizing scenery, all of it. And lost in its beauty, I was hardly aware when the mountain road we were on slowly descended, but suddenly there we were, entering Monte Carlo.

The Ancient and Modern City

It was almost noon. Pam had been there several times before, so she knew just where to go. Without hesitation she drove straight into a parking garage situated discreetly next to a perfectly manicured park with a lovely water pool surrounded by yellow tulips the size of large soup bowls. And then she led me on a short walk down to the water's edge, to the Café de Paris.

An Exquisite Setting

Remember those beautiful bays I described seeing from the mountain road on the way to Monte Carlo? Those formed by the land reaching out to the water but not quite getting their earthen hands together?

Well, the Café de Paris sits at the edge of one of those beautiful bays, adjacent to the Monte Carlo Casino and Hotel de Paris. Together, the three buildings form a sort of semi-circle, with a large fountain in the middle.

And there we sat in the Café's outdoor dining area under the warm spring sun and ate our club sandwiches with a knife and fork in the manner of the people around us

It was an exquisite setting. I loved how the Café, all black and white and tinted glass, sat in modern juxtaposition to the towering casino and hotel – both multi-storied stone structures, elaborately adorned in a mix of Renaissance and Belle Epoque style trim, with tall pillars and wide stairways leading to the grand entrance doors.

And I loved the white tablecloths, all set out with gleaming china and silverware, cut crystal goblets, and silver bud vases with red roses. And I loved how the soft-spoken, highly respectful waiters wore formal white jackets, black pants, and black bow ties.

Also, I loved how our English mingled lyrically with the many foreign languages spoken elegantly by the other patrons around us, all musically accompanied by the tinkling of silverware against dishes and the splashing of water in the fountain out on the parkway.

For two hours, Pam and I lingered over lunch, dining slowly, sipping iced teas, dallying over dessert, thoroughly entertained by the spectacle of one Bentley, Rolls Royce, Bugatti and exotic car after another pulling up to the casino and hotel with their elegant passengers.

And we were also entertained by the comings and goings of the decadently rich dressed in the finest couture money can buy:

Exotic animal skin boots and handbags, exquisite silk dresses and suits; fabulous furs fashioned into coats and jackets - all fashioned by what appeared to be the Michelangelos and Leonardo deVincis of the design world.

The scene was so entertaining, we could have spent the afternoon there at our table. But time was of the essence, so, finally, we paid our bill and set off to explore the city.

The Lovely Bay

Behind the semi-circle of the café and casino and hotel is the lovely bay I mentioned earlier. And after we left the café, Pam led the way to the boardwalk, where some of the world's most expensive sailboats and private yachts were docked in the harbor.

Most of the yachts were mini-cruise ships - four and five-storied luxury homes gleaming white in the sun. Ultra-big, ultra-fancy, ultra-everything, these pampered abodes floated haughtily in the water, at least in my view, barely tolerating their servants, the deck hands who were hard at work scrubbing and polishing their surfaces, adjusting their various types of equipment and tinkering with their satellite systems atop their towering roofs.

And after snapping a million or so pictures, Pam and I set off on foot to see other areas of the city. And very quickly I found Monte Carlo to be the most ultra-rich, ultra-clean city I'd ever been in, one aspiring to the level of art. And adding to its beauty is how it all sits under the auspices of the royal family's digs, high on a bluff above the harbor.

Antibes

A few miles from Monte Carlo, situated at the edge of the sea, lies an ancient town named Antibes. And after exploring Monte Carlo, Pam drove me there to see it.

And once again she knew right where to go. She parked the car in a visitor's lot next to a boat harbor, and then she led the way through a portico into one of the oldest sections of Antibes, where to our delight the village was bustling with activity.

On the sidewalk, a guitarist and singer serenaded the crowd with groovy European music; and dotted here and there a few painters worked at their easels, lending a festive feeling of happiness and creativity to the air.

A few yards away, an open-air market offered the wares of expert artisans - ceramics, wood sculptures, paintings, all manner of decorative and household things, including wonderfully designed and expertly sewn French fashions.

Like honeybees to nectar, we explored the market and indulged in some purchases. Then we bought pastry and coffee and hung out on the street for a while, listening to the music and watching the painters creating truly fine works of art at their easels. And then we set off to explore.

We perused the village's quaint shops, tried on some French fashions, got artistically inspired in a couple of art galleries, got our minds blown in a tiny ceramic shop (that led into a dank but well-lit cave where a storehouse of beautifully painted Italian ceramics lined the shelves), and then we collapsed on a bench in one of the village's piazzas.

We'd treated ourselves to a grand time. And now the sun was beginning its slow but inevitable late-afternoon descent. And not wanting to drive home in the dark, we trudged back to our car "with heavy hearts," as my oft funny sister put it, "knowing that we would probably never live in Monte Carlo."

Back on the Mountain

As much as we didn't want to leave, the two-hour trip back to our condo was surprisingly delightful. Along the way, we stopped and bought bread and fruit at a quaint little store next to an ancient stone church.

And by the time we were back on the mountain road high above the ocean, the sun was suspended just above the horizon, the water was shimmering quietly, and the shadows were growing long across the land.

It was a lovely end to a lovely day. And as we traveled along, we reminisced about the day, and, finally, our conversation turned to the fashions we'd seen in Monte Carlo.

Since arriving in Europe, Pam and I had enjoyed watching 'Fashion TV' at night - a 24-hour channel of runway shows from Paris, Milan, and New York. It was fun to kick back in our pajamas and robes after a long day of exploring and watch a continuous display of the fashion-world's newest designs.

Some of the couture we laughed at; but most of it we loved, especially those fashions designed to make a woman look like a vision of feminine beauty. So, *of course*, it was inevitable that the subject of fashion should come up in our conversation. But what still amazes me is how *God* joined that conversation.......

A Vision of Beauty

Always the Gentleman, God waited until Pam and I had finished talking about the fashions we'd seen that day in Monte Carlo. And when we finally fell silent - Pam driving the car, lost in her own thoughts; me gazing out to sea - He projected a slow-moving picture onto the screen of my mind:

It was of a beautiful young princess, the Bride of Christ, walking on the clouds high above the Earth, ascending to the Marriage Supper of the Lamb.

And from my perspective next to Her, on Her left, I could see the joyful, expectant look on Her pretty young face as She ascended slowly, looking with great anticipation toward the vast, light-filled, open-air Throne of God for the Marriage Celebration.

Her wavy brown hair was pulled up on the sides and tucked under a large gold crown encrusted with diamonds and jewels. And Her wedding gown – well, it was the most beautiful gown I'd ever seen....*or imagined!*

The entire gown was creamy white, and the bodice was fashioned from some kind of Heavenly material that I can't describe. If pearls and diamonds could grow together as one substance, and then woven into fabric, then that might begin to describe it.

Connected to the bodice and flowing down from it at Her waistline, the skirt of the gown was like nothing I'd ever conceived possible! You know how ocean waves coming into shore rise and fall, and move this way and that, melding together to create ever-changing watery shapes?

Well, that's how the train of the Bride's gown moved. Wafting in the breeze behind Her, something like hundreds, maybe thousands, of yards of flower material moved and flowed and melded together, making ever-changing shapes of exquisite white blossoms and buds resembling white roses, gardenias, white peonies, and the like - all flowing behind her like an ocean of flowers, high above the Earth.

Above the train, but connected to it at Her waist, something like hundreds (maybe thousands) of yards of spun crystal netting, wispy and transparent, wafted high in the sky and glinted here and there with the tiniest of tiny flashes of gold in the sunlight.

The Royal Clothing of the Bride of Christ

To say that She was richly and magnificently dressed would be a fantastic understatement! Of greater consequence, though, is what the Holy Spirit said to me as I was preparing for bed that night after Pam and I got back to her condo.

Softly, quietly in my mind, He said: *"The clothing you saw in Monte Carlo today was made from the substance of animals: their blood spilled, their lives sacrificed for their skins. But the Clothing of the Bride of Christ is fashioned from the Substance of the Son of God. He spilled His Blood and sacrificed His Body so that His Bride could be clothed with His Divine Life."*

And I went to bed that night with great happiness and wonder at how Beautifully and Magnificently we will be Clothed as the Bride of Christ on that Glorious Day of the Marriage Supper of the Lamb (Colossians 1:27; First John 3:2)!

"....as the bridegroom rejoices over the bride,
so shall your God rejoice over you."

(Isaiah 62:5)

329

About the Author

A native Californian, KATHY MAY HOSIER is a thankful wife, mother, grandmother, sister, auntie, cousin, and friend to many. She is also an avid reader and loves good literature. And like her sweet husband, Russ, she especially loves God's Word and study books relating to God's Word.

On the musical front, Kathy enjoys a variety of genres, including classical and European groove. And she enjoys activities of all kinds, including painting and writing, traveling, and going to concerts and art galleries. She also loves playing in the ocean and kicking back on the beach, soaking in the rays of the Lord's Presence and communing with Him while watching the waves.

Truly, *"God has given us richly all good things to enjoy"* (First Timothy 6:17). And while Kathy enjoys all good things whenever they come her way, her greatest aim in life since the day she met Jesus in 1971 has been to enjoy His Presence and walk closely with Him. And she is grateful for all the doors the Lord has opened for her over the years to share the Gospel and teach His Word, as well as participate with others in intercessory prayer.

As to this book, Kathy's heart's desire is that all who read it will know more of the Love that Jesus has for each of them personally; and that they would see more clearly how they can experience close fellowship with Him and enjoy the Peace and Power and Victory of His Life as their own by purposely walking with Him according to the seven facets of the Armor of God. And she would love for you to meet up with her on her Chicks for Jesus website.

Finally, Kathy's prayer is that people everywhere who don't yet know Jesus would hear how much He loves them and desires a close relationship with each of them personally. And in response, they would receive His Life and experience His Love and the Beauty of Fellowship with Him - *the King of Kings and Lord of lords* - and be counted among those present as the Bride of Christ on that Glorious Day of the Marriage Supper of the Lamb!

CPSIA information can be obtained
at www.ICGtesting.com
Printed in the USA
BVHW070124261021
619844BV00016B/933